NATIONAL GEOGRAPHIC KiDS

BEGINNER'S UNITED STATES ATLAS

NATIONAL GEOGRAPHIC
WASHINGTON, D.C.

D0002263

Table of Contents

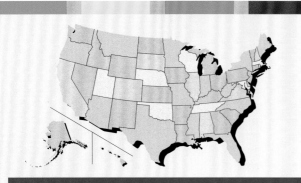

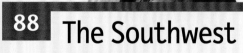

What Is a Map?

An atlas is a collection of maps and pictures. A map is a drawing of a place as it looks from above. It is flat, and it is smaller than the place it shows. Learning to read a map can help you find where you are and where you want to go. **Mapping your home ...**

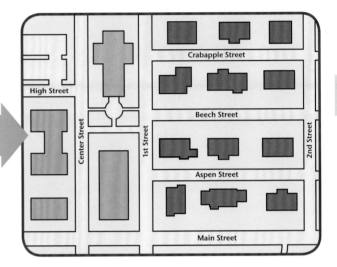

From a bird's-eye view ...
If you were a bird flying directly overhead, you would see only the tops of things. You wouldn't see walls, tree trunks, tires, or feet.

On a large-scale map ... you see places
from a bird's-eye view. But a map uses drawings called symbols to show things on the ground, such as houses or streets. The map of the National Mall in Washington, D.C., on pages 10–11 is an example of a large-scale map.

Finding places on the map

A map can help you get where you want to go. A map helps you read it by showing you north, south, east, and west, plus a key and a scale.

→ A **compass rose** helps you travel in the right direction. It tells you where north (N), south (S), east (E), and west (W) are on your map. Often only a north arrow is used.

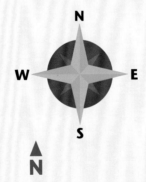

→ A **map key** helps you understand the symbols used by the mapmaker to show things like buildings, towns, or rivers on the map.

★ State capital
• • City or town
▣ Point of interest
--- National trail
•••• Country boundary
······ State boundary
▭ Indian Reservation
▭ State Park
▭ National Park Service
▭ National Forest land

← A **scale** tells you about distance on a map. The scale shows what length on the map represents the labeled distance on the ground.

0 ——————— 100 miles
0 ——————— 100 kilometers

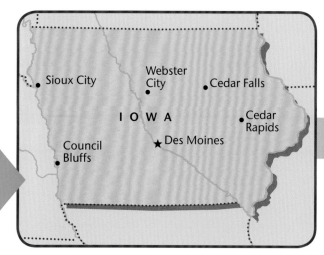

On an intermediate-scale map ...

you see a place from much higher up. A town appears as a tiny dot. You can't see houses, but you can see more of the land around the town. Most maps in this atlas show a whole state with its towns and other special features.

On a small-scale map ... you can see

much more of the country around a state, including other states. But on a small-scale map there is much less detail. You can no longer see most features within the state. Two states—Alaska and Hawai'i—are often shown in separate boxes or on a map of the whole continent, as on pages 6–7.

Map Key for the State Maps in This Atlas

- Aspen ....town of under 25,000 residents
- Frankfort ....town of 25,000 to 99,999
- San Jose ....city of 100,000 to 999,999
- New York ....city of 1,000,000 and over

⊛ National capital
★ State capital
⊐⊏ Pass
▪ Point of interest
+ High point
• Low point
― River
---- Intermittent river
++++ Canal
▪▪▪▪▪ Bridge
----- National trail
••••• Country boundary
•••••••• State boundary
•••••••• Continental Divide
⟋⟍ Lake
⟋⟍ Intermittent lake

Dry lake
Swamp
Glacier
Sand
Lava
Area below sea level
Indian Reservation (I.R.)
State Park (S.P.)
National Park Service
National Historical Park (N.H.P.)
National Lakeshore
National Marine Sanctuary (N.M.S.)
National Monument (NAT. MON.)
National Park (N.P.)
National Preserve (N. PRES.)
National Recreation Area (N.R.A.)
National River
National Scenic Area
National Seashore
National Volcanic Monument
National Forest land
National Grassland (N.G.)

The Land

 Land regions The rugged Sierra Nevada and Rocky Mountains run north to south through the western United States. Between these mountains are dry lands with little vegetation. East of the Rockies are wide, grassy plains and the older, lower Appalachian Mountains.

 Water The Mississippi–Missouri is the longest river system in the United States. The Great Lakes are the largest freshwater lakes in the country.

 Climate The United States has many climate types—from cold Alaska to tropical Hawai'i, with milder climates in the other 48 states.

 Plants The United States has forests where there is plenty of rain. Grasslands cover drier areas.

 Animals There are many kinds of animals—everything from bears and deer to songbirds large and small.

← North America is famous for its **deciduous forests.** Leaves turn fiery colors each fall.

↑ Waves off the Pacific Ocean roll onto a beach along the shore of Moloka'i, one of the islands that make up the state of **Hawai'i.**

↓ Deserts are found in the southwestern part of the United States. This large rock formation, called the Mitten, is in **Monument Valley** in Utah.

← The majestic bald eagle is the national bird of the United States. It is found throughout the country, but about half live in **Alaska.**

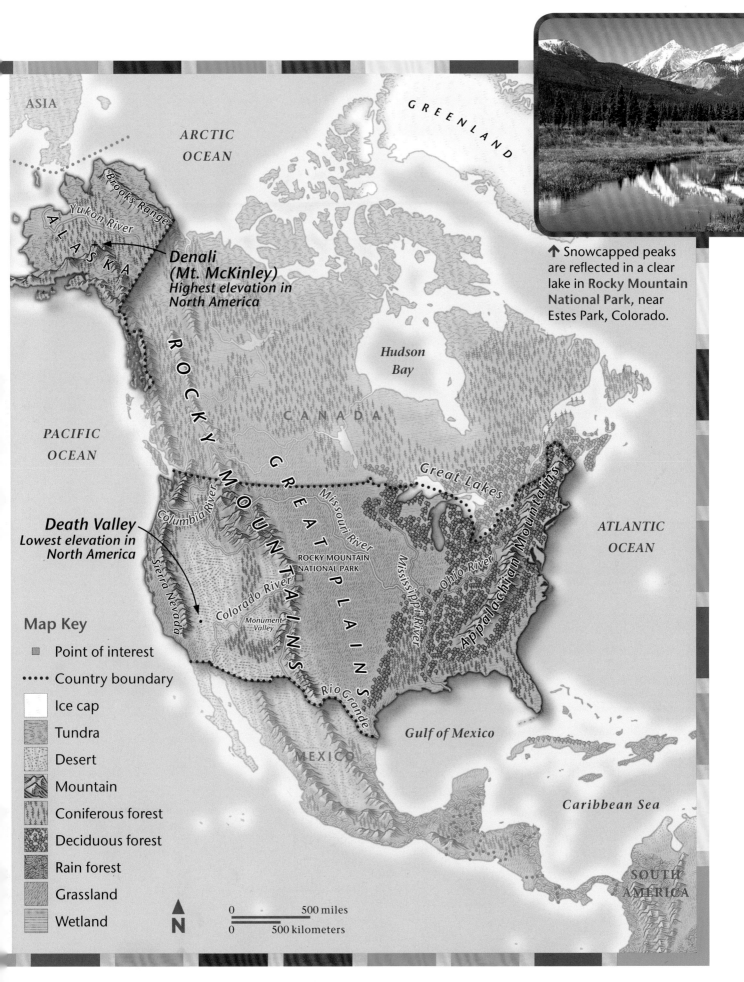

ASIA

ARCTIC OCEAN

GREENLAND

Brooks Range

Yukon River

ALASKA

*Denali
(Mt. McKinley)*
**Highest elevation in
North America**

PACIFIC OCEAN

Hudson Bay

CANADA

R O C K Y   M O U N T A I N S

Death Valley
**Lowest elevation in
North America**

Columbia River

Sierra Nevada

Colorado River

Monument Valley

G R E A T   P L A I N S

Missouri River

ROCKY MOUNTAIN NATIONAL PARK

Mississippi River

Great Lakes

Ohio River

Appalachian Mountains

ATLANTIC OCEAN

↑ Snowcapped peaks
are reflected in a clear
lake in **Rocky Mountain
National Park**, near
Estes Park, Colorado.

Rio Grande

Gulf of Mexico

MEXICO

Caribbean Sea

SOUTH AMERICA

Map Key

- ▪ Point of interest
- ••••• Country boundary
- Ice cap
- Tundra
- Desert
- Mountain
- Coniferous forest
- Deciduous forest
- Rain forest
- Grassland
- Wetland

N

0	500 miles
0	500 kilometers

The People

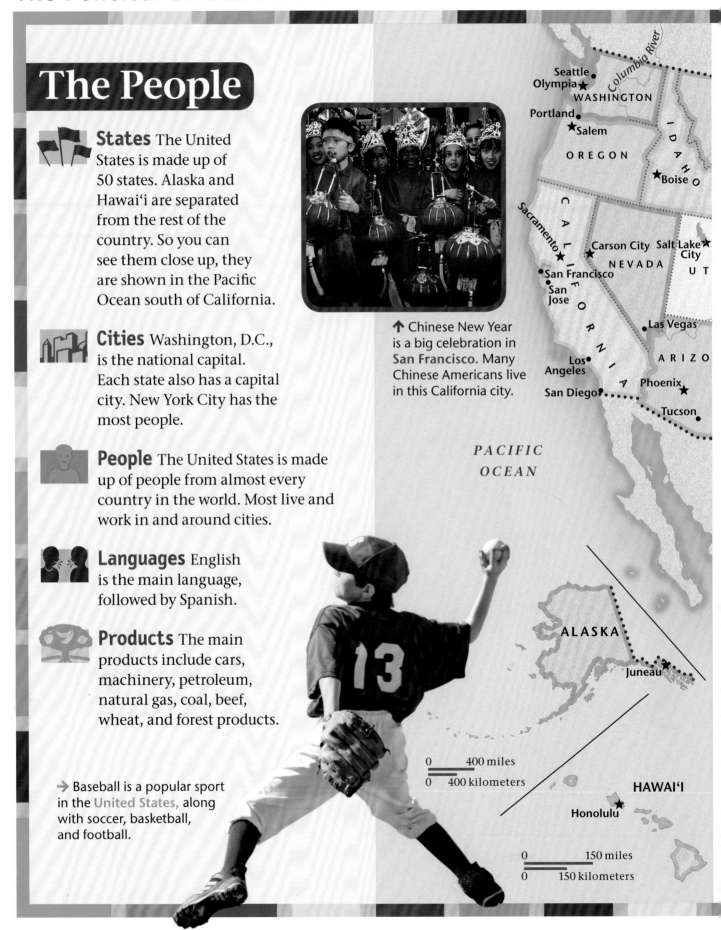

States The United States is made up of 50 states. Alaska and Hawai'i are separated from the rest of the country. So you can see them close up, they are shown in the Pacific Ocean south of California.

Cities Washington, D.C., is the national capital. Each state also has a capital city. New York City has the most people.

People The United States is made up of people from almost every country in the world. Most live and work in and around cities.

Languages English is the main language, followed by Spanish.

Products The main products include cars, machinery, petroleum, natural gas, coal, beef, wheat, and forest products.

→ Baseball is a popular sport in the United States, along with soccer, basketball, and football.

↑ Chinese New Year is a big celebration in San Francisco. Many Chinese Americans live in this California city.

PACIFIC OCEAN

Columbia River

Seattle
Olympia ★
WASHINGTON
Portland
★ Salem
OREGON
IDAHO
★ Boise

CALIFORNIA
Sacramento
★
Carson City
NEVADA
San Francisco
San Jose
Salt Lake City ★
UT

Las Vegas

Los Angeles
San Diego
ARIZO
Phoenix ★
Tucson

ALASKA
Juneau ★

0 — 400 miles
0 — 400 kilometers

HAWAI'I
Honolulu ★

0 — 150 miles
0 — 150 kilometers

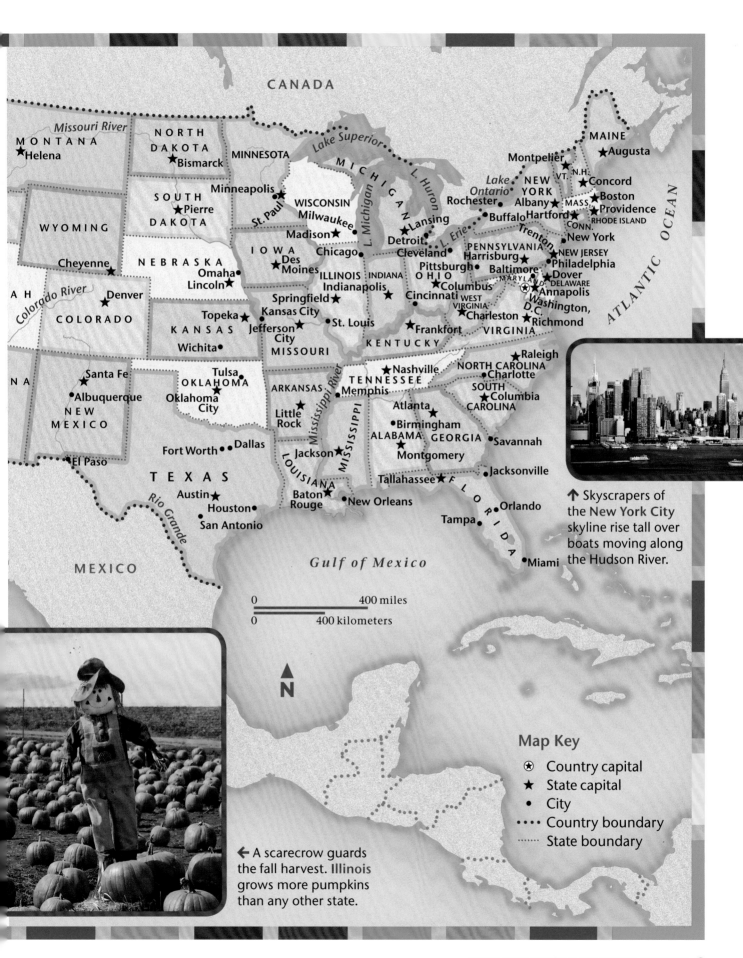

CANADA

Missouri River

MONTANA
★Helena

NORTH DAKOTA
★Bismarck

MINNESOTA

Lake Superior

MICHIGAN

L. Huron

MAINE
★Augusta

Montpelier
VT. N.H.
★Concord

Lake Ontario
NEW YORK
Rochester•
Albany★

MASS.
★Boston
★Providence
RHODE ISLAND

SOUTH DAKOTA
★Pierre

Minneapolis•
St. Paul★

WISCONSIN
Milwaukee•
Madison★

WYOMING

Cheyenne★

Colorado River

Denver★

COLORADO

NEBRASKA
Omaha•
Lincoln★

IOWA
Des Moines★

Buffalo•
Lansing★

Detroit•

L. Michigan

Chicago•

Cleveland•

L. Erie

Hartford★
CONN.

Trenton★

New York•

PENNSYLVANIA
Harrisburg★

NEW JERSEY
Philadelphia•
Dover★

DELAWARE

ILLINOIS
Indianapolis★

INDIANA

OHIO
Columbus★

Cincinnati•

Pittsburgh•

Baltimore•
MARYLAND

Annapolis★

Springfield★

Topeka★
KANSAS

Kansas City•

Jefferson City★

St. Louis•

MISSOURI

Wichita•

WEST VIRGINIA

Charleston★

Frankfort★

KENTUCKY

Washington, D.C.

Richmond★
VIRGINIA

Raleigh★

AH

Santa Fe★
•Albuquerque
NEW MEXICO

NA

Tulsa•
OKLAHOMA
Oklahoma City★

ARKANSAS
Little Rock★

Mississippi River

TENNESSEE
★Nashville
Memphis•

NORTH CAROLINA
•Charlotte

SOUTH CAROLINA
★Columbia

Atlanta★

•Birmingham

El Paso•

Fort Worth•   •Dallas

Jackson★
MISSISSIPPI

ALABAMA   GEORGIA

•Savannah

TEXAS

Rio Grande

Austin★
Houston•
•San Antonio

LOUISIANA

Baton Rouge★   •New Orleans

Montgomery★

Tallahassee★   FLORIDA

•Jacksonville

•Orlando

•Tampa

MEXICO

ATLANTIC OCEAN

Gulf of Mexico

•Miami

↑ Skyscrapers of the New York City skyline rise tall over boats moving along the Hudson River.

0   400 miles
0   400 kilometers

N

Map Key

⊛ Country capital
★ State capital
• City
•••• Country boundary
••••• State boundary

← A scarecrow guards the fall harvest. Illinois grows more pumpkins than any other state.

The National Capital: Washington, D.C.

Land & Water The National Mall, the Potomac River, and the Anacostia River are important land and water features of the District of Columbia.

Statehood The District of Columbia was founded in 1790, but it is not a state.

People & Places The District of Columbia's population is 672,228. Known as Washington, D.C., the city is the seat of the U.S. government.

Fun Fact The flag of the District of Columbia, with three red stars and two red stripes, is based on the shield in George Washington's family coat of arms.

Washington, D.C. Flag

American Beauty Rose
Official Flower

Wood Thrush
Official Bird

➜ The Smithsonian Institution, the world's largest museum, is actually made up of 19 museums and the National Zoo. Established in 1846, it is sometimes called the nation's attic because of its large collections.

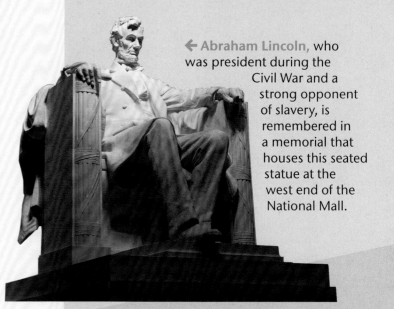

← Abraham Lincoln, who was president during the Civil War and a strong opponent of slavery, is remembered in a memorial that houses this seated statue at the west end of the National Mall.

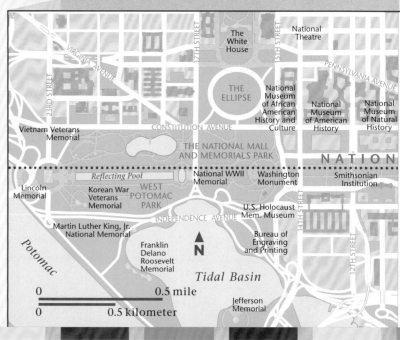

Map labels: 17TH STREET, The White House, National Theatre, 15TH STREET, VIRGINIA AVENUE, 23RD STREET, PENNSYLVANIA AVENUE, THE ELLIPSE, National Museum of African American History and Culture, National Museum of American History, National Museum of Natural History, Vietnam Veterans Memorial, CONSTITUTION AVENUE, THE NATIONAL MALL AND MEMORIALS PARK, NATION, Reflecting Pool, National WWII Memorial, Washington Monument, Smithsonian Institution, Lincoln Memorial, Korean War Veterans Memorial, WEST POTOMAC PARK, U.S. Holocaust Mem. Museum, 14TH STREET, Martin Luther King, Jr. National Memorial, INDEPENDENCE AVENUE, Bureau of Engraving and Printing, 12TH STREET, Potomac, Franklin Delano Roosevelt Memorial, N, Tidal Basin, Jefferson Memorial, 0 — 0.5 mile, 0 — 0.5 kilometer

A giant panda munches on a fresh piece of bamboo on a snowy day at the **National Zoo.** The zoo currently has four giant pandas.

MARYLAND

SHEPHERD PARK

TAKOMA PARK

CHEVY CHASE

BRIGHTWOOD PARK

FORT TOTTEN PARK

MICHIGAN PARK

ROCK CREEK PARK

DISTRICT OF COLUMBIA

SPRING VALLEY

UNIVERSITY HEIGHTS

WOODRIDGE

NORTHWEST

BATTERY KEMBLE PARK

CLEVELAND PARK

NATIONAL ZOOLOGICAL PARK

NORTHEAST

GLOVER-ARCHBOLD PARK

COLUMBIA HEIGHTS

EDGEWOOD

BRENTWOOD VILLAGE

NATIONAL ARBORETUM

VIRGINIA

FOX HALL

GLOVER PARK

ADAMS MORGAN

WESTMINSTER

ECKINGTON

CHESAPEAKE & OHIO NAT. HISTORICAL PARK

LOGAN CIRCLE

TRINIDAD

KALORAMA HEIGHTS

TRUXTON CIRCLE

DEANWOOD

N

GEORGETOWN

DUPONT CIRCLE

STANTON PARK

KINGMAN PARK

CENTRAL NORTHEAST

MARYLAND

CHINATOWN

0 ——— 1 mile
0 ——— 1 kilometer

THE MALL

★

LINCOLN PARK

LINCOLN HEIGHTS

Area enlarged at left

MARSHALL HEIGHTS

•••••• The red dotted lines show how Washington is divided into four quadrants centered around the U.S. Capitol, named Northwest (NW), Northeast (NE), Southwest (SW), and Southeast (SE).

EAST POTOMAC PARK

FORT DUPONT PARK

BENNING HEIGHTS

ANACOSTIA

SOUTHEAST

Anacostia

FAIRLAWN

SOUTHWEST

HILLCREST

Potomac

BARRY FARMS

GARFIELD HEIGHTS

↓ An African-American boy seeks relief from a heat wave in the **District of Columbia.** African Americans make up nearly half of the city's population.

CONGRESS HEIGHTS

WASHINGTON HIGHLANDS

Smithsonian American Art Museum/ National Portrait Gallery

Union Station

7TH STREET
1ST STREET
LOUISANA AVENUE

National Archives

Senate Office Buildings

National Gallery of Art

Capitol Reflecting Pool

NW | NE

AL MALL

U.S. Capitol

BELLVIEW

National Air and Space Museum

Nat. Museum of the American Indian

SW | SE

INDEPENDENCE AVENUE

7TH STREET

House Office Buildings

MARYLAND

▢ Major point of interest
▢ Government building
▢ Built-up area
▢ Park and open area

The Northeast

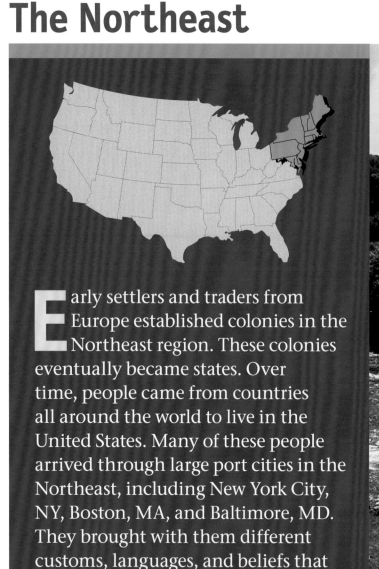

Early settlers and traders from Europe established colonies in the Northeast region. These colonies eventually became states. Over time, people came from countries all around the world to live in the United States. Many of these people arrived through large port cities in the Northeast, including New York City, NY, Boston, MA, and Baltimore, MD. They brought with them different customs, languages, and beliefs that make the Northeast a region of great variety. Today the Northeast region includes the country's financial center, New York City, and its political capital, Washington, D.C.

Water plunges as much as 110 feet (34 m) over the American Falls on the Niagara River near New York's northwestern border with our neighbor Canada. Black bears are common in the forests of the region.

Connecticut

Land & Water Mount Frissell, the Connecticut River, and Long Island Sound are important land and water features of Connecticut.

Statehood Connecticut became the 5th state in 1788.

People & Places Connecticut's population is 3,590,886. Hartford is the state capital. The largest city is Bridgeport.

Fun Fact The sperm whale, Connecticut's state animal, is known for its massive head. Its brain is larger than that of any other creature known to have lived on Earth.

Connecticut State Flag

Mountain Laurel
State Flower

Robin
State Bird

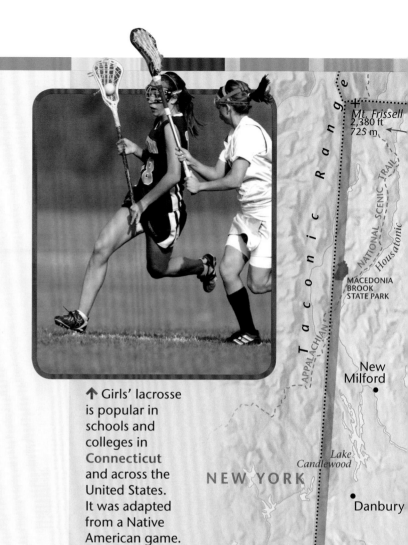

↑ Girls' lacrosse is popular in schools and colleges in **Connecticut** and across the United States. It was adapted from a Native American game.

← The *Charles W. Morgan,* launched in 1841 and now docked in **Mystic Seaport,** is the only remaining wooden whaling ship in the world.

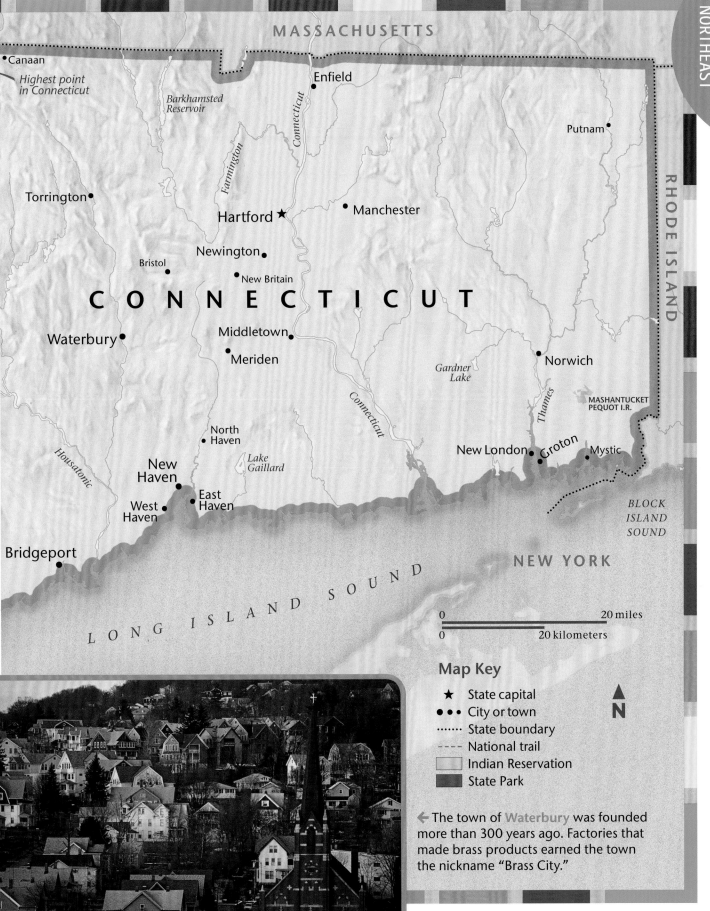

MASSACHUSETTS

• Canaan
Highest point in Connecticut

Enfield

Barkhamsted Reservoir

Connecticut

Putnam

Farmington

Torrington •

Hartford ★   • Manchester

Newington •

Bristol •
            • New Britain

C O N N E C T I C U T

Middletown •

Waterbury •

Meriden •

Gardner Lake

Norwich •

Connecticut

North
Haven •

Lake Gaillard

Thames

MASHANTUCKET
PEQUOT I.R.

New Haven

Housatonic

East
Haven

New London • Groton • Mystic

West
Haven

Bridgeport •

*BLOCK
ISLAND
SOUND*

NEW YORK

L O N G   I S L A N D   S O U N D

RHODE ISLAND

| 0 | 20 miles |
| 0 | 20 kilometers |

Map Key

★ State capital
••• City or town
······ State boundary
----- National trail
▢ Indian Reservation
▪ State Park

N

← The town of **Waterbury** was founded more than 300 years ago. Factories that made brass products earned the town the nickname "Brass City."

DELAWARE

Delaware

Land & Water The Barrier Islands, Cypress Swamp, and Delaware Bay are important land and water features of Delaware.

Statehood Delaware became the 1st state in 1787.

People & Places Delaware's population is 945,934. Dover is the state capital. The largest city is Wilmington.

Fun Fact Each year contestants bring pumpkins and launching machines to the Punkin Chunkin World Championship in Bridgeville to see who can toss their big orange squash the farthest.

↑ The Delmarva Peninsula, with more than 1,500 poultry growers, is a major producing area for chickens. The industry's trade association is located in **Georgetown**.

→ Patriotic boys wave American flags at a Delaware motorsports track near **Delmar**. Racing fans have come to the tracks since they opened in 1963.

↓ Brightly colored umbrellas dot **Bethany Beach**. Sun, sand, and surf attract thousands of vacationers each year to Delaware's shore.

DECEMBER 7, 1787

Delaware State Flag

Peach Blossom
State Flower

Blue Hen Chicken
State Bird

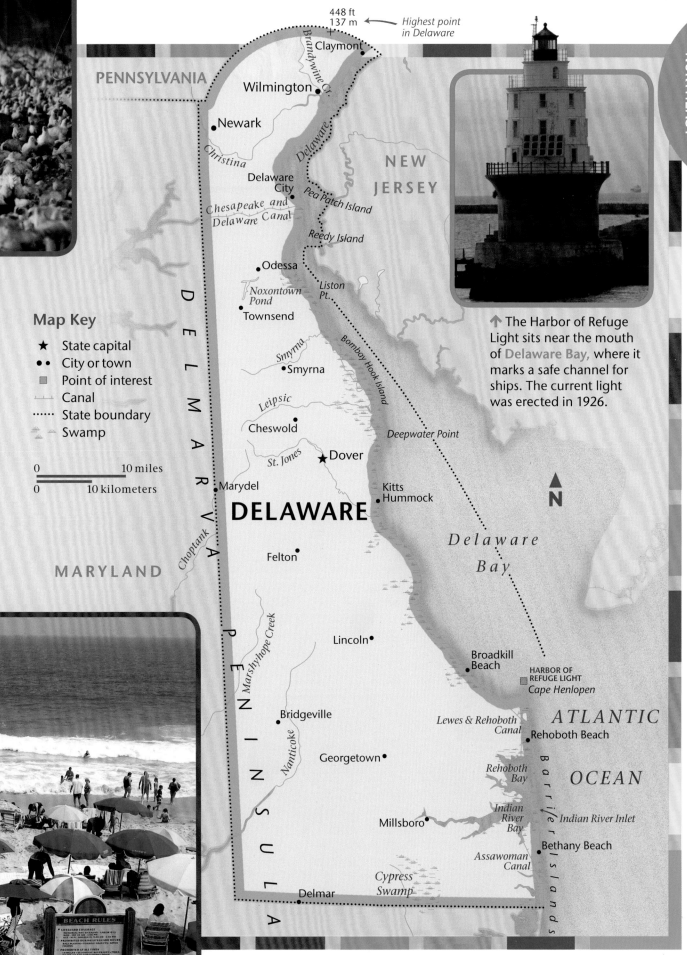

448 ft
137 m ← Highest point
in Delaware

PENNSYLVANIA

Claymont

Wilmington

Newark

Brandywine Cr.

Christina

Delaware

NEW
JERSEY

Delaware
City

*Chesapeake and
Delaware Canal*

Pea Patch Island

Reedy Island

Odessa

*Noxontown
Pond*

Liston
Pt.

Townsend

Bombay Hook Island

Map Key

★ State capital
•• City or town
▢ Point of interest
⊢ Canal
⋯ State boundary
≈ Swamp

0	10 miles
0	10 kilometers

Smyrna

Smyrna

Leipsic

Cheswold

Deepwater Point

St. Jones

★ Dover

Marydel

DELAWARE

Kitts
Hummock

*Delaware
Bay*

N

MARYLAND

Choptank

Felton

Lincoln

Broadkill
Beach

HARBOR OF
REFUGE LIGHT
Cape Henlopen

The Harbor of Refuge
Light sits near the mouth
of Delaware Bay, where it
marks a safe channel for
ships. The current light
was erected in 1926.

Marshyhope Creek

Bridgeville

*Lewes & Rehoboth
Canal*

Rehoboth Beach

ATLANTIC

Georgetown

Nanticoke

*Rehoboth
Bay*

OCEAN

Millsboro

*Indian
River
Bay*

Indian River Inlet

Bethany Beach

*Assawoman
Canal*

Delmar

*Cypress
Swamp*

DELMARVA PENINSULA

Barrier Islands

THE NORTHEAST **17**

Maine

 Land & Water The Appalachian Mountains, Mount Katahdin, and the Gulf of Maine are important land and water features of Maine.

 Statehood Maine became the 23rd state in 1820.

 People & Places Maine's population is 1,329,328. Augusta is the state capital. The largest city is Portland.

 Fun Fact During the last ice age, glaciers carved hundreds of bays and inlets along Maine's shoreline and created some 2,000 islands off the coast.

↑ More than 60 lighthouses line Maine's rocky coastline, warning ships of danger. The oldest lighthouse, Portland Head Light, is located at Cape Elizabeth.

← Each year Rockland hosts the Maine Lobster Festival. This celebration of the state's popular seafood delicacy attracts visitors from far and near.

↓ Moose are North America's largest deer, averaging six feet (2 m) tall at the shoulders. This female stands knee-deep in grass near Rangeley Lake.

Maine State Flag

White Pine Cone and Tassel
State Flower

Chickadee
State Bird

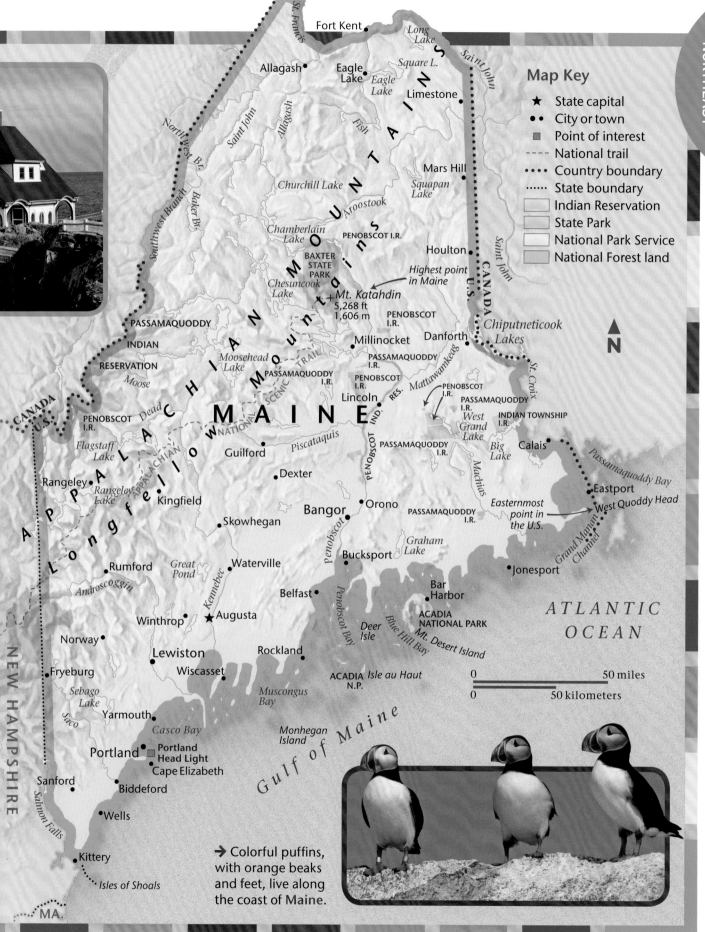

Map Key

★ State capital
•• City or town
■ Point of interest
---- National trail
•••• Country boundary
····· State boundary
☐ Indian Reservation
☐ State Park
☐ National Park Service
☐ National Forest land

Fort Kent
St. Francis
Long Lake
Saint John
Allagash
Eagle Lake
Eagle Lake
Square L.
Limestone
Northwest Br.
Saint John
Fish
Mars Hill
Churchill Lake
Squapan Lake
Aroostook
Allagash
Baker Br.
Southwest Branch
Chamberlain Lake
PENOBSCOT I.R.
BAXTER STATE PARK
Houlton
CANADA
U.S.
Chesuncook Lake
Saint John
Highest point in Maine
Mt. Katahdin
5,268 ft
1,606 m
PENOBSCOT I.R.
Chiputneticook Lakes
N
PASSAMAQUODDY
Danforth
INDIAN
Millinocket
PASSAMAQUODDY I.R.
St. Croix
RESERVATION
Moosehead Lake
PENOBSCOT I.R.
Mattawamkeag
PENOBSCOT I.R.
West Grand Lake
PASSAMAQUODDY I.R.
INDIAN TOWNSHIP
Moose
PASSAMAQUODDY I.R.
Lincoln
PENOBSCOT IND. RES.
CANADA
U.S.
Dead
MAINE
Big Lake
Calais
Passamaquoddy Bay
PENOBSCOT I.R.
PENOBSCOT IND.
PASSAMAQUODDY I.R.
Flagstaff Lake
NATIONAL
Piscataquis
Guilford
Machias
Easternmost point in the U.S.
Eastport
Rangeley
APPALACHIAN
Rangeley Lake
SCENIC TRAIL
Dexter
PASSAMAQUODDY I.R.
West Quoddy Head
Kingfield
Longfellow
Orono
Bangor
PASSAMAQUODDY I.R.
Grand Manan Channel
Skowhegan
Penobscot
Graham Lake
Jonesport
MOUNTAINS
Rumford
Great Pond
Waterville
Bucksport
Androscoggin
Bar Harbor
ATLANTIC OCEAN
Belfast
Penobscot Bay
ACADIA NATIONAL PARK
Kennebec
Deer Isle
Blue Hill Bay
Mt. Desert Island
Norway
Winthrop
★ Augusta
Rockland
Lewiston
Wiscasset
ACADIA N.P.
Isle au Haut
0   50 miles
Fryeburg
Muscongus Bay
0   50 kilometers
Sebago Lake
Saco
Yarmouth
Casco Bay
Monhegan Island
Gulf of Maine
Portland
Portland Head Light
Sanford
Cape Elizabeth
Biddeford
Salmon Falls
Wells
NEW HAMPSHIRE
Kittery
Isles of Shoals
MA.

→ Colorful puffins, with orange beaks and feet, live along the coast of Maine.

Maryland

 Land & Water The Appalachian Mountains, Potomac River, and Chesapeake Bay are important land and water features of Maryland.

 Statehood Maryland became the 7th state in 1788.

 People & Places Maryland's population is 6,006,401. Annapolis is the state capital. The largest city is Baltimore.

 Fun Fact The name of Baltimore's professional football team—the Ravens—may have been inspired by a poem written by the famous American author Edgar Allan Poe, who lived in Baltimore in the mid-1800s.

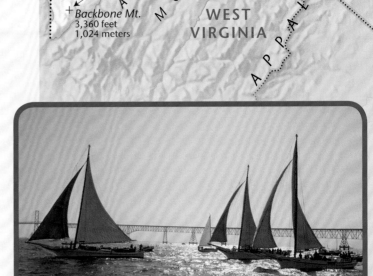

↑ Sailing is a popular pastime on Maryland's Chesapeake Bay. In the background, the **Bay Bridge** stretches 4.3 miles (6.9 km) across the waters of the bay.

Maryland State Flag

Black-Eyed Susan
State Flower

Northern (Baltimore) Oriole
State Bird

↑ Since the early 1700s, Baltimore, near the upper Chesapeake Bay, has been a major seaport and a focus of trade, industry, and immigration.

Map labels:
Cumberland
Youghiogheny
Deep Creek Lake
Highest point in Maryland
+ Backbone Mt. 3,360 feet 1,024 meters
Allegheny Mountains
N. Branch
S. Branch
Chesapeake and Ohio Canal
Potomac
WEST VIRGINIA
APPALACHIAN

PENNSYLVANIA

Hagerstown

ANTIETAM
NATIONAL
BATTLEFIELD

CATOCTIN
MOUNTAIN
PARK

Elkton

Aberdeen

Reisterstown

Monocacy

Frederick

Edgewood

Towson

Parkville

Baltimore

Sassafras

Susquehanna

Chester

Dundalk

M
O
U
N
T
A
I
N
S

APPALACHIAN NATIONAL SCENIC TRAIL

CHESAPEAKE AND

HARPERS
FERRY
N.H.P.

Gaithersburg

Patuxent

Columbia

MARYLAND

OHIO CANAL N.H.P.

Rockville

Silver
Spring

Severn

Bay Bridge

Kent
Island

DELAWARE

VIRGINIA

Potomac

Bethesda

Bowie

Annapolis

Eastern
Bay

Easton

P
i
e
d
m
o
n
t

D.C.

Suitland

N

Choptank

Cambridge

St. Charles

Patuxent

C
h
e
s
a
p
e
a
k
e

B
a
y

Salisbury

Ocean
City

Map Key

★ State capital
••• City or town
— Canal
▪▪▪ Bridge
- - - National trail
⋯ State boundary
▨ National Park Service

Lexington Park

Potomac

*Bloodsworth
Island*

*Fishing
Bay*

Nanticoke

Pocomoke

I
N
S
U
L
A

ASSATEAGUE
ISLAND
NATIONAL
SEASHORE

Chincoteague Bay

0   40 miles
0   40 kilometers

Point
Lookout

*Smith
Island*

Tangier Sound

*Assateague
Island*

*Pocomoke
Sound*

VIRGINIA

A
T
L
A
N
T
I
C
O
C
E
A
N

↓ Blue crabs,
found in the
waters of
Chesapeake Bay,
were important
in the diet of
Native Americans.

→ Wild ponies have
lived on **Assateague
Island** since the 1600s.
Today more than 300
ponies live on this
Atlantic barrier island.

MASSACHUSETTS

Massachusetts

 Land & Water The Berkshires, Cape Cod, and Nantucket Sound are important land and water features of Massachusetts.

 Statehood Massachusetts became the 6th state in 1788.

 People & Places Massachusetts's population is 6,794,422. Boston is the state capital and the largest city.

 Fun Fact In 1891 James Naismith invented the game of basketball as a form of physical activity. Today the Basketball Hall of Fame is located in Springfield in his honor.

Massachusetts State Flag

 Chickadee
State Bird

Mayflower
State Flower

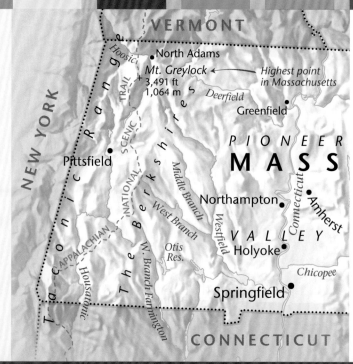

VERMONT

North Adams
Mt. Greylock ← Highest point in Massachusetts
3,491 ft
1,064 m
Deerfield
Greenfield

NEW YORK

Pittsfield

PIONEER
MASS

Northampton
Amherst

VALLEY
Holyoke

Chicopee

Springfield

CONNECTICUT

The Berkshires

Taconic Range

Hoosic

TRAIL

SCENIC

NATIONAL

APPALACHIAN

Housatonic

Middle Branch
West Branch
Westfield
Otis Res.
W. Branch Farmington

↑ Fenway Park in **Boston** is home to the Red Sox major league baseball team. The park was named for a Boston neighborhood known as the Fens.

↓ Cranberries are a major agricultural crop in Massachusetts, which produces 25 percent of the cranberries grown in the United States. An annual cranberry harvest festival is held in **Wareham**.

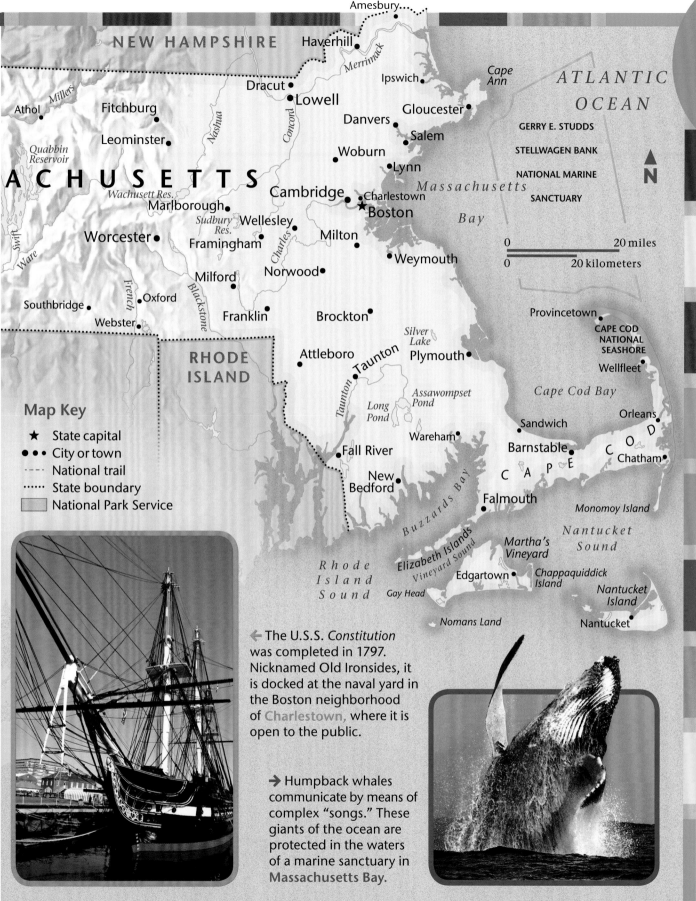

NEW HAMPSHIRE

ATLANTIC OCEAN

Cape Ann

Miller's

Athol •
Fitchburg •
Leominster •

Quabbin Reservoir

Wachusett Res.

ACHUSETTS

Amesbury....

Haverhill •
Dracut •
• Lowell
Danvers •
Salem •
Woburn •
• Lynn
Cambridge •
Charlestown •
★ Boston

Nashua
Concord
Merrimack

Ipswich •
Gloucester •

Massachusetts Bay

GERRY E. STUDDS
STELLWAGEN BANK
NATIONAL MARINE
SANCTUARY

N

Marlborough •
Wellesley •
Worcester •
Framingham •
Milford •

Sudbury Res.
Charles

Milton •
Weymouth •

0   20 miles
0   20 kilometers

Southbridge •
Oxford •
Webster •

French
Blackstone

Franklin •
Brockton •

Swift
Ware

RHODE ISLAND

Attleboro •
Taunton Taunton •
Plymouth •

Silver Lake

Assawompset Pond

Provincetown •

CAPE COD NATIONAL SEASHORE

Wellfleet •

Cape Cod Bay

Map Key

★ State capital
• • • City or town
- - - National trail
⋯⋯ State boundary
▢ National Park Service

Long Pond

Wareham •

Fall River •

New Bedford •

Sandwich •
Barnstable •

Orleans •

C A P E   C O D

Chatham •

Buzzards Bay

Falmouth •

Monomoy Island

Nantucket Sound

Rhode Island Sound

Elizabeth Islands
Vineyard Sound

Edgartown •

Martha's Vineyard

Chappaquiddick Island

Nantucket Island

Gay Head

Nantucket •

Nomans Land

← The U.S.S. *Constitution* was completed in 1797. Nicknamed Old Ironsides, it is docked at the naval yard in the Boston neighborhood of Charlestown, where it is open to the public.

→ Humpback whales communicate by means of complex "songs." These giants of the ocean are protected in the waters of a marine sanctuary in Massachusetts Bay.

New Hampshire

Land & Water The White Mountains, Mount Washington, and the Merrimack River are important land and water features of New Hampshire.

Statehood New Hampshire became the 9th state in 1788.

People & Places New Hampshire's population is 1,330,608. Concord is the state capital. The largest city is Manchester.

Fun Fact The first potato grown in the United States was planted in 1719 in Londonderry on the Common Field, now known simply as the Commons.

⬆ A golden dome topped by a war eagle rises above New Hampshire's State House in **Concord**. The pale granite building was completed in 1819.

⬅ Bitter cold and heavy snow are common in the White Mountains of New Hampshire, where snow tubing and skiing are popular winter sports.

New Hampshire State Flag

⬇ **Mount Washington** rises above trees rich with autumn colors. But soon winter will arrive, bringing some of the most extreme weather in the world.

Purple Lilac
State Flower

Purple Finch
State Bird

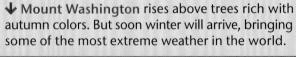

Map Key

★ State capital
• • • City or town
– – – National trail
• • • • Country boundary
• • • • • State boundary
State Park
National Forest land

First Connecticut Lake

Lake Francis

CANADA
U.S.

Colebrook

Connecticut

North Stratford

Umbagog Lake

APPALACHIAN

Groveton

Lancaster

Moore Reservoir

Mt. Washington
6,288 ft 1,917 m

FRANCONIA NOTCH S.P.

White

CRAWFORD NOTCH S.P.

MOUNTAINS

Highest point in New Hampshire

Haverhill

VERMONT

APPALACHIAN

National

NEW
HAMPSHIRE

Squam Lake

Bearcamp

Center Sandwich

Ossipee

MAINE

Hanover

Newfound Lake

Pemigewasset

Bristol

Lake Winnipesaukee

Laconia

Sunapee Lake

Franklin

Winnipesaukee

Suncook Lakes

Salmon Falls

MT. SUNAPEE S.P.

Pittsfield

Rochester

Merrimack

Charlestown

Contoocook

Dover

Concord

Piscataqua

Walpole

Contoocook

Lamprey

Great Bay

Isles of Shoals

Manchester

Ashuelot

Londonderry

Derry

Hampton

PISGAH S.P.

Peterborough

Merrimack

ATLANTIC
OCEAN

Connecticut

Winchester

New Ipswich

Salem

Merrimack

Nashua

MASSACHUSETTS

↑ A black bear cub clings to the trunk of a tree in a **New Hampshire** forest.

N

0   20 miles
0   20 kilometers

NEW JERSEY

New Jersey

 Land & Water The Kittatinny Mountains, Cape May, and the Delaware River are important land and water features of New Jersey.

Statehood New Jersey became the 3rd state in 1787.

 People & Places New Jersey's population is 8,958,013. Trenton is the state capital. The largest city is Newark.

Fun Fact The first dinosaur skeleton found in North America was excavated at Haddonfield in 1858. It was named *Hadrosaurus* in honor of its discovery site.

↑ Sandy beaches on the Atlantic coast of New Jersey attract vacationers from near and far. Roller coasters are just one of the exciting rides in amusement parks along the shore.

← Street names, such as Boardwalk and Park Place, in the popular board game Monopoly are taken from actual street names in Atlantic City.

↓ The skylines of Jersey City (foreground) and New York City (in the distance at right) glow in the evening light. Jersey City, the second largest city in the state, is home to many large corporations.

New Jersey State Flag

American Goldfinch
State Bird

Violet
State Flower

High Point
1,803 ft
550 m

Highest point in New Jersey

NEW YORK

Ringwood

Wanaque Reservoir

Sparta

Lake Hopatcong

Ridgewood

Paterson

Hackensack

Musconetcong

MORRISTOWN N.H.P.

Newark

New York

Jersey City

Elizabeth

Ellis Island

Woodbridge

GATEWAY N.R.A.

Lower Bay

Phillipsburg

LOWER DELAWARE

Round Valley Res.

Raritan

Edison

Sandy Hook

SCENIC &

New Brunswick

Sandy Hook Bay

Sandy Hook

GATEWAY N.R.A.

RECREATIONAL RIVER

East Brunswick

Delaware

N E W

Red Bank

Long Branch

Delaware & Raritan Canal

Manalapan

Asbury Park

Mercerville

Trenton ★

J E R S E Y

Point Pleasant

PENNSYLVANIA

Lakewood

Toms

Willingboro

Pennsauken

Camden

Toms River

Seaside Heights

Cherry Hill

Haddonfield

NEW JERSEY

Barnegat Bay

Mullica

PINELANDS

Long Beach Island

Glassboro

Hammonton

NATIONAL RESERVE

Ship Bottom

Little Egg Harbor

Pennsville

Maurice

GREAT EGG HARBOR NATIONAL SCENIC AND RECREATIONAL RIVER

Great Egg Harbor

Beach Haven

DELAWARE

Salem

Vineland

Great Bay

Bridgeton

Cohansey

Millville

Atlantic City

Tuckahoe

Ventnor City

Somers Point

Ocean City

A T L A N T I C

O C E A N

N

Delaware Bay

CAPE MAY

Cape May Court House

Cape May

Victorian-style houses line a street in **Cape May**. The town is a national historic landmark and the country's oldest seashore resort.

Southern Jersey
FAMOUS
Tomatoes
$2.50
The real deal!!

New Jersey, known as the Garden State, is a leading producer of fresh fruits and vegetables.

Map Key

★ State capital
●●● City or town
⊔ Canal
--- National trail
····· State boundary
Swamp
☐ National Park Service

0 _____ 20 miles
0 _____ 20 kilometers

New York

 Land & Water The Adirondack Mountains, the Finger Lakes, and the Hudson River are important land and water features of New York.

 Statehood New York became the 11th state in 1788.

 People & Places New York's population is 19,795,791. Albany is the state capital. The largest city is New York City.

Fun Fact The Erie Canal, built in the 1820s, connected Buffalo to the Hudson River at Albany, allowing ships to travel from the Atlantic Ocean to the Great Lakes. The canal contributed to the growth of New York City as a major trade center.

New York State Flag

Eastern Bluebird
State Bird

Rose
State Flower

← Fresh, juicy apples are on display at a roadside stand near **Chautauqua.** New York is the second largest producer of apples in the United States.

CANADA
U.S.

ST. REGIS I.R.

Malone

Plattsburgh

St. Lawrence

Ogdensburg

Lake Champlain

Thousand Islands

Lake Placid

Raquette

A d i r o n d a c k

→ Mt. Marcy ✛
5,344 ft
1,629 m

Highest point in New York

ADIRONDACK

CANADA
U.S.

Watertown

M o u n t a i n s

Lake George

Black

PARK

VERMONT

Hudson

Oswego

Oswego

Oneida Lake

Rome

Utica

Glens Falls

Great Sacandaga Lake

Saratoga Springs

Erie Canal

Mohawk

Erie Canal

Schenectady

M O U N T A I N S

Syracuse

ONONDAGA INDIAN RESERVATION

Troy

Taconic Range

Auburn

Cooperstown

Albany ★

Seneca Lake

ger **L a k e s**

Cayuga Lake

Catskill

Hudson

MASSACHUSETTS

Keuka Lake

Ithaca

N E W   Y O R K

A P P A L A C H I A N

Hudson

Watkins Glen

Susquehanna

W. Br. Delaware

Catskill Mountains

Binghamton

Chemung

Elmira

CATSKILL PARK

✛ Slide Mt.
4,180 ft
1,274 m

V A N I A

Susquehanna

E. Branch

UPPER DELAWARE SCENIC AND RECREATIONAL RIVER

CONNECTICUT

RHODE ISLAND

← Once seriously polluted, the **Gowanus Canal,** in the Brooklyn area of New York City, has been undergoing cleaning efforts. Here, people canoe and enjoy the view from the water.

Newburgh

Poughkeepsie

Middletown

Delaware

NATIONAL SCENIC

TRAIL

Block Island Sound

Montauk Point

Long Island Sound

Spring Valley

APPALACHIAN

New Rochelle

Huntington

Southampton

Yonkers

Brentwood

New York

New York Harbor → □ Gowanus Canal

Freeport

FIRE ISLAND NATIONAL SEASHORE

Long Island

NEW JERSEY

Staten Island

GATEWAY N.R.A.

Long Beach

ATLANTIC OCEAN

↑ Standing in **New York Harbor,** the Statue of Liberty, a gift from the people of France, is a symbol of freedom and democracy.

▲ N

Map Key

★ State capital
●●●● City or town
■ Point of interest
⊥ Canal
---- National trail
•••• Country boundary

······ State boundary
☐ Indian Reservation
☐ State Park
☐ National Park Service
☐ National Forest land

| 0 | | 50 miles |
| 0 | | 50 kilometers |

Pennsylvania

 Land & Water The Allegheny Mountains, the Pocono Mountains, and the Susquehanna River are important land and water features of Pennsylvania.

 Statehood Pennsylvania became the 2nd state in 1787.

People & Places Pennsylvania's population is 12,802,503. Harrisburg is the state capital. The largest city is Philadelphia.

 Fun Fact The town of Hershey is known as the Chocolate Capital of the World. The Hershey Company exports its chocolate candies to some 70 countries around the world.

Pennsylvania State Flag

Mountain Laurel
State Flower

Ruffed Grouse
State Bird

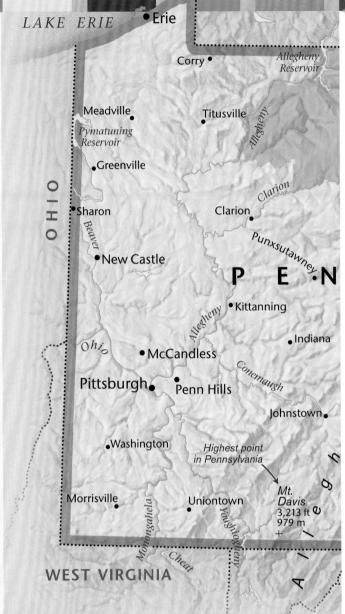

LAKE ERIE

Erie

Corry

Allegheny Reservoir

Meadville

Titusville

Pymatuning Reservoir

OHIO

Greenville

Clarion

Sharon

Clarion

Punxsutawney

New Castle

P · E · N

Allegheny

Kittanning

Ohio

Indiana

Beaver

McCandless

Conemaugh

Pittsburgh

Penn Hills

Johnstown

Washington

Highest point in Pennsylvania

Morrisville

Uniontown

Mt. Davis
3,213 ft
979 m

Monongahela

Youghiogheny

Allegh

WEST VIRGINIA

Cheat

Map Key

★ State capital
●●●● City or town
- - - National trail
.... State boundary
▢ National Park Service
▢ National Forest land

APPALACHIAN TRAIL

← The **Appalachian Trail** stretches across more than 2,000 miles (3,200 km) from Maine to Georgia. The trail passes through 14 states, including Pennsylvania.

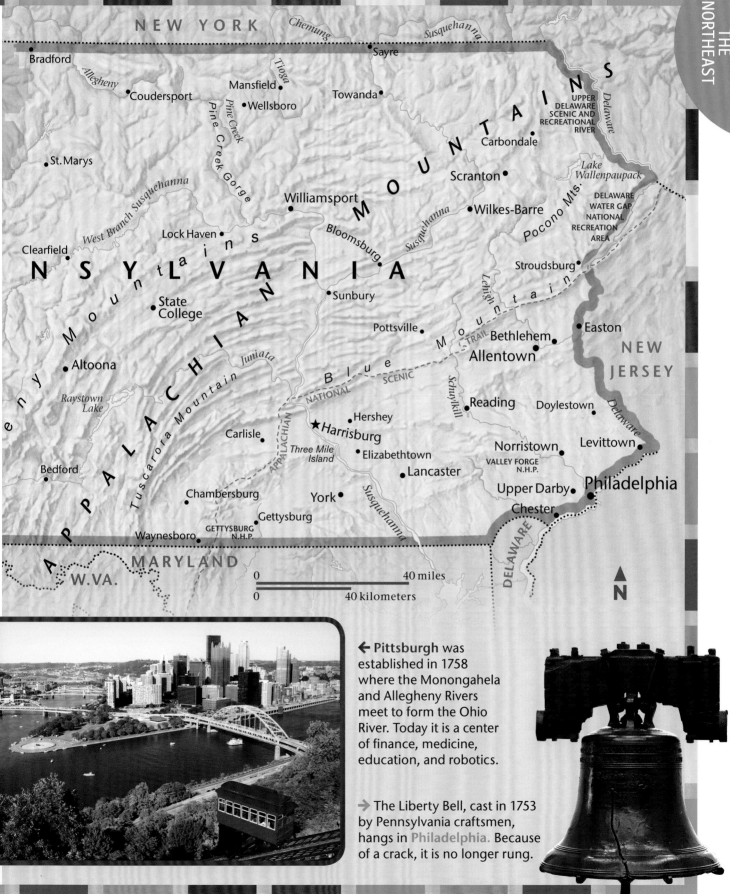

NEW YORK

Chemung

Susquehanna

Bradford

Allegheny

Coudersport

Mansfield

Tioga

Wellsboro

Sayre

Towanda

Pine Creek

Pine Creek Gorge

St. Marys

MOUNTAINS

Carbondale

Scranton

UPPER DELAWARE SCENIC AND RECREATIONAL RIVER

Delaware

Lake Wallenpaupack

Williamsport

West Branch Susquehanna

Lock Haven

Bloomsburg

Susquehanna

Wilkes-Barre

Pocono Mts.

DELAWARE WATER GAP NATIONAL RECREATION AREA

Clearfield

N S Y L V A N I A

Mountains

Stroudsburg

Lehigh

Sunbury

State College

Pottsville

Blue

Mountain

TRAIL

Bethlehem

Easton

Allentown

NEW JERSEY

Altoona

Juniata

APPALACHIAN

NATIONAL

SCENIC

Schuylkill

Reading

Doylestown

Delaware

Raystown Lake

Tuscarora Mountain

Carlisle

★ Harrisburg

Hershey

Three Mile Island

Norristown

Levittown

Bedford

APPALACHIAN

Elizabethtown

Lancaster

VALLEY FORGE N.H.P.

Upper Darby

Philadelphia

Chambersburg

York

Susquehanna

Chester

Waynesboro

Gettysburg

GETTYSBURG N.H.P.

DELAWARE

A

W. VA.

MARYLAND

0   40 miles

0   40 kilometers

N

← **Pittsburgh** was established in 1758 where the Monongahela and Allegheny Rivers meet to form the Ohio River. Today it is a center of finance, medicine, education, and robotics.

→ The Liberty Bell, cast in 1753 by Pennsylvania craftsmen, hangs in Philadelphia. Because of a crack, it is no longer rung.

The Northeast

Rhode Island

Land & Water Block Island and Narragansett Bay, with its many islands, are important land and water features of Rhode Island.

Statehood Rhode Island became the 13th state in 1790.

People & Places Rhode Island's population is 1,056,298. Providence is the state capital and the largest city.

Fun Fact Rhode Island is the smallest U.S. state in size. It measures just 48 miles (77 km) from north to south and 37 miles (60 km) from east to west.

↑ Sailing is a popular sport in Rhode Island. This boat is in full sail on a late summer day on Narragansett Bay.

← The North Lighthouse on the northern tip of **Block Island** still warns ships of dangerous waters. The building, constructed in 1867, does not have a typical lighthouse design.

Rhode Island State Flag

Violet
State Flower

Rhode Island Red
State Bird

↓ Rhode Island has cold, snowy winters. Skaters enjoy ice-skating on City Center public rink in front of the historic city hall in Providence.

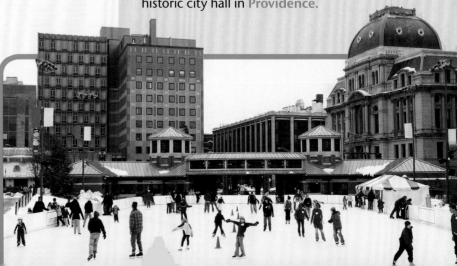

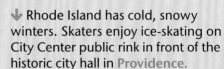

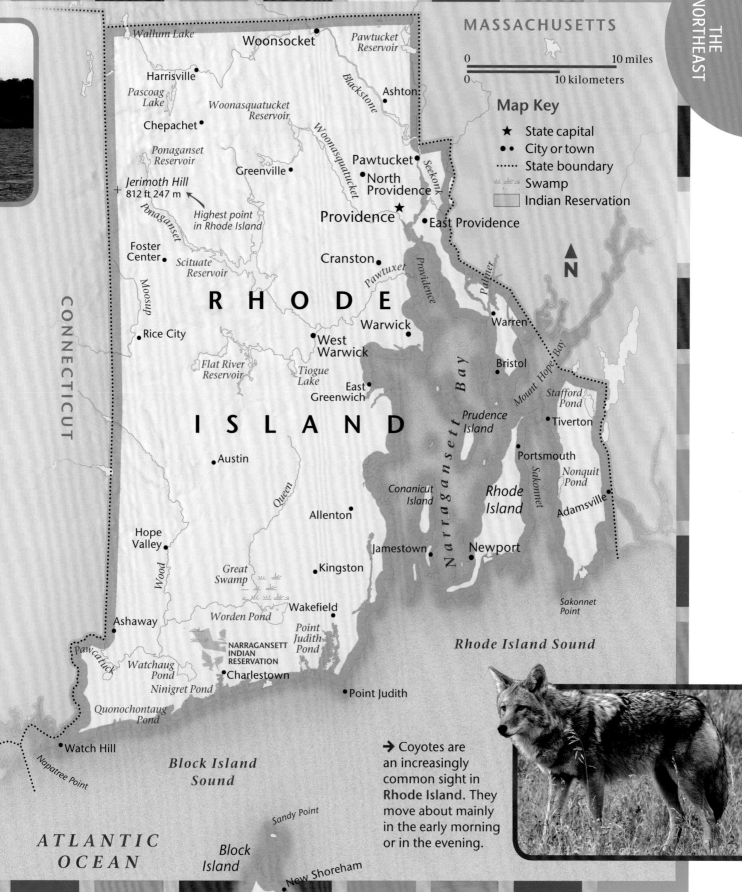

MASSACHUSETTS

0 — 10 miles
0 — 10 kilometers

Map Key

★ State capital
•● City or town
∙∙∙∙ State boundary
Swamp
Indian Reservation

Wallum Lake

Woonsocket

Pawtucket Reservoir

Harrisville

Pascoag Lake

Blackstone

Ashton

Chepachet

Woonasquatucket Reservoir

Ponaganset Reservoir

Woonasquatucket

Pawtucket

Greenville

North Providence

Seekonk

+ Jerimoth Hill
812 ft 247 m

Providence ★

East Providence

Highest point in Rhode Island

Ponaganset

Foster Center

Scituate Reservoir

Cranston

Pawtuxet

Providence

R H O D E

Moosup

Palmer

Rice City

Warwick

Warren

West Warwick

Flat River Reservoir

Tiogue Lake

Bristol

Mount Hope Bay

Stafford Pond

East Greenwich

I S L A N D

Narragansett Bay

Prudence Island

Tiverton

Portsmouth

Sakonnet

Nonquit Pond

Austin

Conanicut Island

Rhode Island

Adamsville

Queen

Allenton

CONNECTICUT

Hope Valley

Wood

Jamestown

Newport

Kingston

Sakonnet Point

Great Swamp

Wakefield

Rhode Island Sound

Worden Pond

Point Judith Pond

Ashaway

Pawcatuck

NARRAGANSETT INDIAN RESERVATION

Charlestown

Watchaug Pond

Ninigret Pond

●Point Judith

Quonochontaug Pond

●Watch Hill

Napatree Point

Block Island Sound

→ Coyotes are an increasingly common sight in **Rhode Island**. They move about mainly in the early morning or in the evening.

Sandy Point

ATLANTIC OCEAN

Block Island

New Shoreham

Vermont

Land & Water The Green Mountains, Lake Champlain, and the Connecticut River are important land and water features of Vermont.

Statehood Vermont became the 14th state in 1791.

People & Places Vermont's population is 626,042. Montpelier is the state capital. The largest city is Burlington.

Fun Fact From the end of the Revolutionary War until 1791, Vermont was an independent republic with its own government and money. It even thought about uniting with Canada.

↑ Vermont ice cream is famous worldwide. The headquarters of Ben & Jerry's in Burlington is the number one tourist attraction in the state.

Vermont State Flag

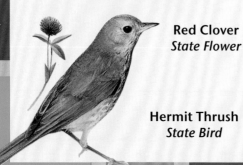

Red Clover
State Flower

Hermit Thrush
State Bird

↑ People collect the sap of maple trees, which is boiled to make maple sugar and syrup. Maple production is celebrated each year at a festival in Tunbridge.

CANADA
U.S.

Richford

Lake Memphremagog

Newport

Canaan

N

0 ——————— 40 miles
0 ——————— 40 kilometers

North Hero Island

Saint Albans

Missisquoi

Barton

Clyde

Lake Willoughby

Island Pond

Connecticut

Map Key

★ State capital
•• City or town
--- National trail
•••• Country boundary
••••• State boundary
National Park Service
National Forest land

South Hero Island

Lake Champlain

Lamoille

Mt. Mansfield
4,393 ft
1,339 m

Morrisville

Passumpsic

Moose

Highest point in Vermont

Burlington

Shelburne

Winooski

Waterbury

St. Johnsbury

Moore Reservoir

NEW HAMPSHIRE

Vergennes

★ Montpelier

Barre

Wells River

Middlebury

V E R M O N T

Otter Creek

Lake Dunmore

Mad

White

M o u n t a i n s

A P P A L A C H I A N   M O U N T A I N S

Tunbridge

Brandon

Lake Bomoseen

A P P A L A C H I A N   N A T I O N A L   S C E N I C   T R A I L

Hartford

→ With as much as 100 inches (254 cm) of snow each winter, Vermont's Green Mountains provide plenty of opportunities for snowboarding and skiing.

Poultney

Fair Haven

Poultney

Rutland

+ Killington Peak
4,235 ft 1,291 m

MARSH-BILLINGS-
ROCKEFELLER N.H.P.

Windsor

Black

Metlowee

A P P A L A C H I A N   R a n g e

G r e e n

↓ Farming has a long history in Vermont. The state produces dairy products, fruits and vegetables, maple syrup, and Christmas trees.

N E W   Y O R K

Springfield

Batten Kill

Arlington

Stratton Mt.
3,936 ft
1,200 m

Bellows Falls

Somerset Reservoir

West

T a c o n i c   R a n g e

L O N G   T R A I L

+ Mt. Snow
3,556 ft
1,084 m

Putney

Hoosic

Bennington

Brattleboro

Connecticut

Harriman Reservoir

Deerfield

M A S S A C H U S E T T S

The Southeast

The Southeast region of the United States is full of variety, both in its landscape and in its history. The Appalachian Mountains are old and worn down. The coastal margins are marked by barrier islands and wetlands. And in the western part of the region, the Mississippi River flows out through a broad delta into the Gulf of Mexico. The region, with roots in agriculture, suffered great destruction during the Civil War, but today it is a part of the Sunbelt, where cities are growing rapidly and the economy is shifting to high-tech industries.

Live oak trees, some hundreds of years old, form a natural arch across a country road in Georgia. These trees, draped in Spanish moss, are common in the coastal Southeast. Flamingos are a familiar sight in parks in Florida.

ALABAMA

Alabama

Land & Water The Appalachian Mountains, the Cumberland Plateau, and Mobile Bay are important land and water features of Alabama.

Statehood Alabama became the 22nd state in 1819.

People & Places Alabama's population is 4,858,979. Montgomery is the state capital. The largest city is Birmingham.

Fun Fact In Magnolia Springs, on Mobile Bay, mail is delivered by boat. This city has the country's only year-round, all-water mail route used by the U.S. Postal Service.

↑ Southern Alabama has a narrow coastline fronting the Gulf of Mexico. The beach resort of **Gulf Shores** is a popular tourist destination.

↑ A welder repairs a boat in **Bayou La Batre** on Alabama's Gulf coast. The town is a center for shipbuilding and seafood processing.

↓ This old railroad bridge, built in 1839, was a toll bridge across the **Tennessee River**. Today it is a pedestrian bridge.

Alabama State Flag

Northern Flicker *State Bird*

Camellia *State Flower*

Map Key

★ State capital
• • • City or town
· · · · State boundary
▢ National Park Service
▢ National Forest land

The bobwhite quail is common throughout Alabama. It builds its nest on the ground and lives on a diet of seeds.

TENNESSEE

Pickwick Lake
Wilson Lake
Florence
Tennessee
Madison
Huntsville
Wheeler Lake
Decatur
Guntersville Lake
Russellville
Bear Creek
Cullman
Mulberry Fork
Locust Fork
Cumberland Plateau
Weiss Lake
Gadsden
APPALACHIAN MTS.
LITTLE RIVER CANYON NATIONAL PRESERVE
Lewis Smith Lake
Winfield
Anniston
Cheaha Mt. 2,407 ft 734 m +
Birmingham
Bessemer Hoover
Talladega
Highest point in Alabama
Tuscaloosa
Tombigbee
Sipsey
Black Warrior
Coosa
Chattahoochee
GEORGIA
Clanton
Lake Martin
West Point Lake
A L A B A M A
York
Cahaba
Selma
Auburn
Tallapoosa
Phenix City
B l a c k
Alabama
★ Montgomery
Tuskegee
B e l t
Union Springs
Thomasville
William "Bill" Dannelly Reservoir
Greenville
Conecuh
Troy
Eufaula
Walter F. George Reservoir
Monroeville
Pea
Andalusia
Choctawhatchee
Dothan
Chattahoochee
Tombigbee
Alabama
Atmore
Conecuh
Geneva
Mobile
Tensaw
Prichard
Mobile
Perdido
Bayou La Batre
Fairhope
Magnolia Springs
Mobile Bay
FLORIDA
Mississippi Sound
Dauphin Island
Gulf Shores
Intracoastal Waterway
GULF OF MEXICO

N

0 ___ 50 miles
0 ___ 50 kilometers

MISSISSIPPI

The Southeast

Arkansas

Land & Water The Ouachita Mountains, the Ozark Plateau, and the Mississippi River are important land and water features of Arkansas.

Statehood Arkansas became the 25th state in 1836.

People & Places Arkansas has a population of 2,978,204. Little Rock is the state capital and the largest city.

Fun Fact In 1924 Crater of Diamonds State Park near Murfreesboro yielded the largest natural diamond ever found in the United States. The stone, called "Uncle Sam," weighed more than 40 carats.

↑ Located in the River Market District of **Little Rock**, the Museum of Discovery offers children interactive experiences in science, technology, engineering, and math.

Arkansas State Flag

Apple Blossom
State Flower

Mockingbird
State Bird

↑ A farmer in eastern Arkansas checks the progress of his rice crop. The state is a leading producer of rice.

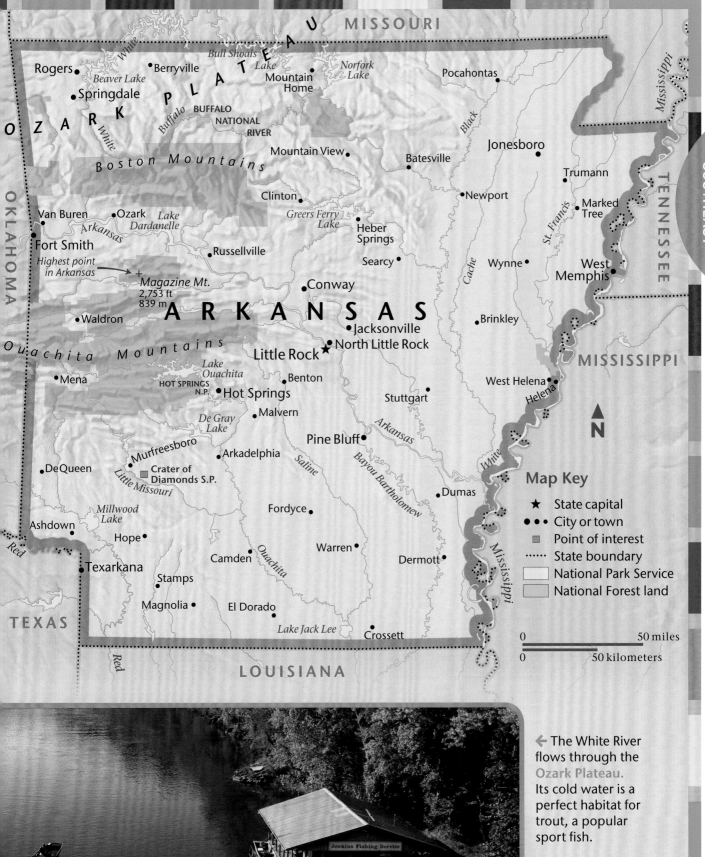

MISSOURI

OZARK PLATEAU

Rogers
Berryville
Beaver Lake
Springdale
White
Bull Shoals Lake
Mountain Home
Norfork Lake
Pocahontas

Buffalo
BUFFALO NATIONAL RIVER
White

Boston Mountains

Mountain View
Batesville
Jonesboro
Trumann
Black

Clinton
Newport
Marked Tree

Van Buren
Ozark
Lake Dardanelle
Greers Ferry Lake
Heber Springs
Searcy
Wynne
St. Francis
West Memphis

Arkansas
Fort Smith

Highest point in Arkansas
Magazine Mt. 2,753 ft 839 m

Russellville

Conway

Cache

Brinkley

A R K A N S A S

Waldron

Ouachita Mountains

Jacksonville
Little Rock
North Little Rock

MISSISSIPPI

Mena
Lake Ouachita
HOT SPRINGS N.P.
Hot Springs
Benton
Stuttgart
West Helena
Helena

De Gray Lake
Malvern
Arkansas

Murfreesboro
Crater of Diamonds S.P.
Little Missouri
Arkadelphia
Saline
Pine Bluff
Bayou Bartholomew
White

DeQueen

Millwood Lake
Hope
Fordyce
Dumas

Ashdown
Camden
Ouachita
Warren
Dermott

Red
Texarkana
Stamps

Magnolia
El Dorado
Lake Jack Lee
Crossett

TEXAS

Red

LOUISIANA

Mississippi

OKLAHOMA

TENNESSEE

N

Map Key

★ State capital
••• City or town
■ Point of interest
••••• State boundary
National Park Service
National Forest land

0   50 miles
0   50 kilometers

← The White River flows through the Ozark Plateau. Its cold water is a perfect habitat for trout, a popular sport fish.

Jenkins Fishing Service

FLORIDA

Florida

A L A B A M A

Highest point → ✛ Britton Hill
in Florida   345 ft
                 105 m

Perdido

Pensacola •   Fort Walton
                   Beach

GULF ISLANDS
NATIONAL SEASHORE   Panama
                         City •

Land & Water The Florida Keys, the Everglades, and Lake Okeechobee are important land and water features of Florida.

Statehood Florida became the 27th state in 1845.

People & Places Florida's population is 20,271,272. Tallahassee is the state capital. The largest city is Jacksonville.

⬇ The manatee is the state marine mammal of **Florida**. It averages ten feet (3 m) in length and can weigh 1,000 pounds (450 kg).

Fun Fact Everglades National Park is home to rare and endangered species such as the American crocodile, the Florida panther, and the West Indian manatee.

⬇ NASA's new Space Launch System, the most powerful rocket in history, will lift off from **Kennedy Space Center** in 2018.

Florida State Flag

Orange Blossom
State Flower

Mockingbird
State Bird

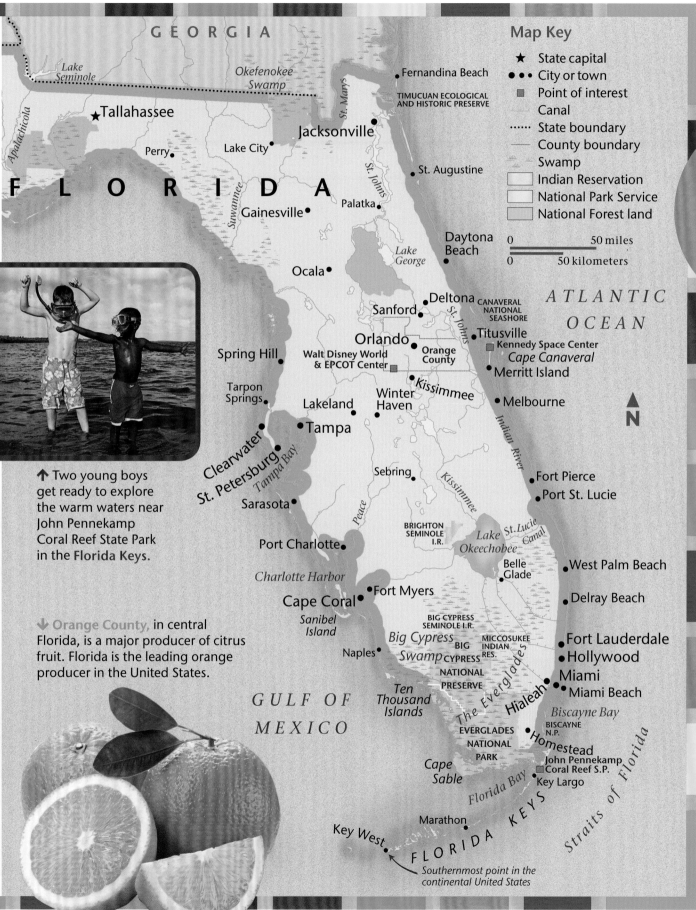

GEORGIA

Map Key

★ State capital
●●● City or town
■ Point of interest
― Canal
···· State boundary
― County boundary
Swamp
Indian Reservation
National Park Service
National Forest land

0 _____ 50 miles
0 _____ 50 kilometers

Lake Seminole

Okefenokee Swamp

★ Tallahassee

Apalachicola

Perry

Lake City

Jacksonville

Fernandina Beach

TIMUCUAN ECOLOGICAL AND HISTORIC PRESERVE

St. Marys

FLORIDA

St. Augustine

Suwannee

Gainesville

Palatka

St. Johns

Daytona Beach

Ocala

Lake George

Deltona

Sanford

CANAVERAL NATIONAL SEASHORE

ATLANTIC OCEAN

St. Johns

Orlando

Titusville

Kennedy Space Center

Cape Canaveral

Spring Hill

Walt Disney World & EPCOT Center

Orange County

Merritt Island

Tarpon Springs

Kissimmee

Winter Haven

Melbourne

Lakeland

Tampa

Clearwater

Sebring

Indian River

St. Petersburg

Tampa Bay

Fort Pierce

Port St. Lucie

Sarasota

Peace

Kissimmee

BRIGHTON SEMINOLE I.R.

St. Lucie Canal

Port Charlotte

Charlotte Harbor

Lake Okeechobee

Belle Glade

West Palm Beach

Delray Beach

Fort Myers

Cape Coral

Sanibel Island

BIG CYPRESS SEMINOLE I.R.

MICCOSUKEE INDIAN RES.

Fort Lauderdale

Big Cypress Swamp

BIG CYPRESS

Hollywood

Naples

NATIONAL PRESERVE

The Everglades

Miami

Miami Beach

GULF OF MEXICO

Ten Thousand Islands

Hialeah

Biscayne Bay

EVERGLADES NATIONAL PARK

BISCAYNE N.P.

Homestead

Cape Sable

John Pennekamp Coral Reef S.P.

Straits of Florida

Florida Bay

Key Largo

FLORIDA KEYS

Marathon

Key West

Southernmost point in the continental United States

↑ Two young boys get ready to explore the warm waters near John Pennekamp Coral Reef State Park in the **Florida Keys**.

↓ **Orange County,** in central Florida, is a major producer of citrus fruit. Florida is the leading orange producer in the United States.

Georgia

Land & Water The Sea Islands, the Okefenokee Swamp, and the Savannah River are important land and water features of Georgia.

Statehood Georgia became the 4th state in 1788.

People & Places Georgia's population is 10,214,860. Atlanta is the state capital and the largest city.

Fun Fact The Georgia Aquarium in Atlanta is the largest aquarium in the world. It features more than 100,000 animals living in more than eight million gallons (30.3 million L) of water.

← Built for the 1996 Olympic Games, Centennial Olympic Park in Atlanta is the site of festivals and community events that attract an estimated three million visitors each year.

→ Nearly half the peanut crop in the United States is grown in Georgia. Sylvester is the peanut capital of the world.

↓ Alligators, which can live more than 50 years, are found in marshes, rivers, and swamps, including those in the Okefenokee National Wildlife Refuge.

Georgia State Flag

Cherokee Rose
State Flower

Brown Thrasher
State Bird

TENNESSEE

NORTH CAROLINA

APPALACHIAN MOUNTAINS

Blue Ridge

Highest point
in Georgia

CHICKAMAUGA &
CHATTANOOGA
N.M.P.

Dalton

Brasstown Bald
4,784 ft 1,458 m

APPALACHIAN
NATIONAL
SCENIC
TRAIL

N

Map Key

★ State capital
●●● City or town
- - - National trail
····· State boundary
Swamp
National Park Service
National Forest land
National Wildlife Refuge

Toccoa

Hartwell L.

Savannah

THE
SOUTHEAST

Rome

Etowah

CHATTAHOOCHEE RIVER
N.R.A.

Lake
Sidney Lanier

Gainesville

Richard B.
Russell Lake

SOUTH
CAROLINA

KENNESAW MOUNTAIN
N.B.P.

Roswell

Marietta

Smyrna

Athens

J. Strom Thurmond
Reservoir

↓ Peaches, a leading
state crop, were intro-
duced to Georgia's
Sea Islands in 1571.

Atlanta

East Point

Washington

Carrollton

Chattahoochee

Lake
Oconee

Augusta

Griffin

Lake
Sinclair

West Point
Lake

La Grange

Waynesboro

Flint

Macon

GEORGIA

Warner
Robins

Ogeechee

Statesboro

Savannah

Columbus

Vidalia

Savannah

FORT PULASKI
N.M.

Americus

Ocmulgee

Oconee

Hinesville

Ossabaw
Island

St. Catherines
Island

Walter F. George
Reservoir

Fitzgerald

Altamaha

Jesup

Sapelo Island

St. Simons Island

Albany

Sylvester

Tifton

St. Simons Island

Jekyll Island

St. Andrew Sound

Chattahoochee

Flint

Alapaha

Waycross

Cumberland Island

CUMBERLAND ISLAND
NATIONAL SEASHORE

Lake
Seminole

Thomasville

Valdosta

Okefenokee

Okefenokee
Swamp

OKEFENOKEE
NATIONAL
WILDLIFE
REFUGE

Kingsland

SEA ISLANDS

St. Marys

ATLANTIC
OCEAN

0   50 miles
0   50 kilometers

FLORIDA

Suwannee

ALABAMA

The Southeast

Kentucky

Land & Water Mammoth Cave, Lake Cumberland, and the Ohio River are important land and water features of Kentucky.

Statehood Kentucky became the 15th state in 1792.

People & Places Kentucky's population is 4,425,092. Frankfort is the state capital. The largest city is Louisville.

Fun Fact The song "Happy Birthday to You," one of the most popular songs in the English language, was written in 1893 by two sisters living in Louisville.

Kentucky State Flag

Goldenrod
State Flower

Cardinal
State Bird

→ Shaker Village in **Pleasant Hill** preserves the culture and history of this important social movement.

← Abraham Lincoln, the 16th U.S. president, was born near **Hodgenville**. His profile appears on the penny.

↓ The setting sun turns the sky red over **Cave Run Lake**. The lake is a popular vacation spot because of its natural beauty.

Map Key

★ State capital
••• City or town
····· State boundary
)⊂ Pass
▢ National Park Service
▨ National Forest land

N

0   50 miles
0   50 kilometers

OHIO

Covington
Florence

Ohio

Licking

Williamstown

Maysville

Vanceburg

Ashland

Ohio

WEST VIRGINIA

La Grange

Kentucky

Flemingsburg

Licking

B L U E G R A S S

Frankfort

Paris

Big Sandy

INDIANA

Louisville

Jeffersontown

Georgetown

Lexington

Cave Run Lake

Winchester

R E G I O N

Salt

Pleasant Hill

Red

Kentucky

Prestonsburg

Tug Fork

Radcliff

Richmond

Jackson

Pikeville

Ohio

Owensboro

Rough River Lake

Elizabethtown

Hodgenville

K E N T U C K Y

Cumberland Plateau

Leitchfield

Nolin River Lake

Campbellsville

Mount Vernon

Highest point in Kentucky

Rockcastle

VIRGINIA

Green

Green River Lake

Somerset

London

Cumberland Mountain

MAMMOTH CAVE NATIONAL PARK

Cave City

Black Mt.
4,145 ft
1,263 m

Bowling Green

Glasgow

Cumberland

Lake Cumberland

Pine

Cumberland

A P P A L A C H I A N

Barren River Lake

Franklin

Albany

CUMBERLAND GAP N.H.P.

Cumberland Mts.

M O U N T A I N S

Dale Hollow Lake

BIG SOUTH FORK NAT. RIVER & REC. AREA

Middlesboro

Cumberland Gap

TENNESSEE

← Riders in colorful jerseys astride powerful race horses charge out of the starting gate during a race in **Kentucky**. The state is a major producer of Thoroughbred race horses.

LOUISIANA

Louisiana

Land & Water Driskill Mountain, Lake Pontchartrain, and the Mississippi River are important land and water features of Louisiana.

Statehood Louisiana became the 18th state in 1812.

People & Places Louisiana's population is 4,670,724. Baton Rouge is the state capital. The largest city is New Orleans.

Fun Fact The Louisiana state capitol building in Baton Rouge is the tallest of all the state capitols. It is a limestone skyscraper that stands 450 feet (137 m) tall and has 34 stories!

Louisiana State Flag

Magnolia
State Flower

Brown Pelican
State Bird

↑ Musicians practice on a park bench in New Orleans as they wait for one of the city's Mardi Gras parades to begin.

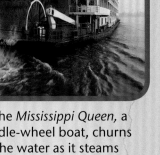

↑ The *Mississippi Queen*, a paddle-wheel boat, churns up the water as it steams along the Mississippi River between Baton Rouge and New Orleans.

Springhill
Red
Caddo Lake
Caddo Black Bayou Preserve
Bossier City
Shreveport
Lake Bistineau
Mansfield
Red
Toledo Bend Reservoir
Natchitoches
Many
Leesville
De Ridder
Sabine
Lake Charles
TEXAS
Sabine Lake
Calcasieu Lake

← Louisiana is a leading producer of shrimp in the United States. Most of it is harvested from the Barataria-Terrebonne estuary of the Mississippi River.

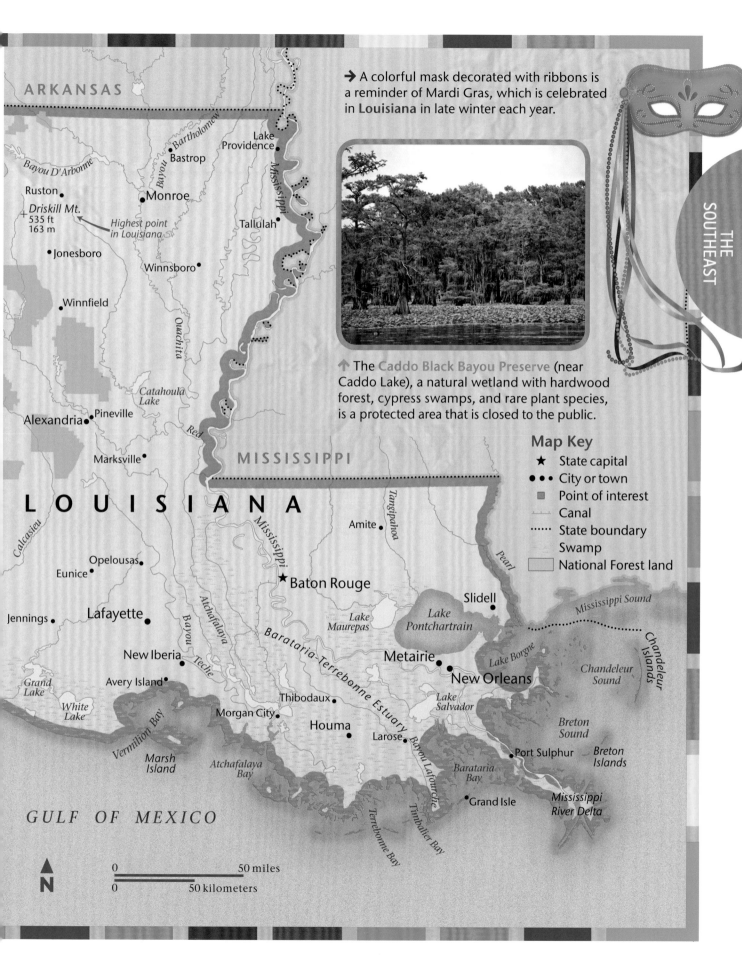

ARKANSAS

Bayou D'Arbonne

Bayou Bartholomew

Lake Providence

Bastrop

Ruston

Monroe

+ Driskill Mt.
535 ft
163 m
Highest point in Louisiana

Tallulah

Jonesboro

Winnsboro

Winnfield

Ouachita

Catahoula Lake

Alexandria • Pineville

Marksville •

Red

MISSISSIPPI

L O U I S I A N A

Calcasieu

Opelousas

Eunice

Lafayette

Jennings

New Iberia

Avery Island

Grand Lake

White Lake

Vermilion Bay

Marsh Island

Atchafalaya

Bayou Teche

Atchafalaya Bay

Morgan City

Thibodaux

Houma

Larose

Barataria-Terrebonne Estuary

Bayou Lafourche

Timbalier Bay

Terrebonne Bay

Mississippi

Tangipahoa

Amite

★ Baton Rouge

Lake Maurepas

Lake Pontchartrain

Pearl

Slidell

Metairie

New Orleans

Lake Borgne

Lake Salvador

Barataria Bay

Grand Isle

Port Sulphur

Mississippi Sound

Chandeleur Islands

Chandeleur Sound

Breton Sound

Breton Islands

Mississippi River Delta

GULF OF MEXICO

➡ A colorful mask decorated with ribbons is a reminder of Mardi Gras, which is celebrated in **Louisiana** in late winter each year.

⬆ The Caddo Black Bayou Preserve (near Caddo Lake), a natural wetland with hardwood forest, cypress swamps, and rare plant species, is a protected area that is closed to the public.

Map Key

★ State capital
●●● City or town
■ Point of interest
━ Canal
···· State boundary
  Swamp
  National Forest land

N

0 _____ 50 miles
0 _____ 50 kilometers

Mississippi

Land & Water The Mississippi Petrified Forest, the Tennessee-Tombigbee Waterway, and the Mississippi River are important land and water features of Mississippi.

Statehood Mississippi became the 20th state in 1817.

People & Places Mississippi's population is 2,992,333. Jackson is the state capital and the largest city.

Fun Fact Jim Henson, creator of Kermit the Frog, Miss Piggy, Big Bird, and other famous Muppets, was born in Greenville.

Mississippi State Flag

Mockingbird
State Bird

Magnolia
State Flower

↑ Mississippi is the leading producer of catfish in the United States. A part of the **Mississippi River Valley** known as the Delta is the main producing area.

↑ Two bridges stretch across the Mississippi River in the city of **Vicksburg.** The river is home to more than 400 species of wildlife.

↓ Children play in a tidal pool on a **Biloxi** beach as the sun sets. Barrier islands separate the city from the Gulf of Mexico.

TENNESSEE

Southaven

Corinth · *Pickwick Lake*

Woodall Mt.
806 ft, 246 m +

ARKANSAS

Senatobia · · Booneville

Sardis Lake

Little Tallahatchie

Oxford · · New Albany

Yocona

Clarksdale · **Tupelo** ·

Water Valley ·

Shelby · Houston ·

Yalobusha · Aberdeen

Ruleville · West Point ·

D E L T A *Tombigbee*

Winona · **Columbus** ·

Greenville · Indianola ·

Big Black

Yazoo Kosciusko · · Louisville

M I S S I S S I P P I

Yazoo City · · Philadelphia

Carthage · **MISSISSIPPI CHOCTAW INDIAN RESERVATION**

MISSISSIPPI PETRIFIED FOREST *Ross Barnett Reservoir* *Pearl*

Ridgeland · · Forest **Meridian** ·

Vicksburg · Brandon · Newton

Jackson ★

ALABAMA

Leaf Quitman ·

Crystal Springs ·

Hazlehurst · · Magee

Collins ·

Natchez · Brookhaven · Ellisville · Waynesboro ·

Pearl **Hattiesburg** ·

Homochitto McComb · Columbia

Centreville · Lucedale ·

LOUISIANA

Wiggins · *Black Creek* *Pascagoula*

Gulfport · **Biloxi** ·
Bay St. Louis · *Mississippi Sound* **Pascagoula**

GULF ISLANDS NAT. SEASHORE

GULF OF MEXICO

Mississippi

Coldwater

Tallahatchie

Mississippi

Deer Creek

Yazoo

Tennessee

Tennessee-Tombigbee Waterway

Highest point in Mississippi

Chickasawhay

Tombigbee

↑ Farmers in **Mississippi** plant more than a million acres (405,000 ha) of cotton each year. Technology and improved seeds keep production high.

Map Key

★ State capital
·· City or town
▪ Point of interest
─ Canal
···· State boundary
▨ Indian Reservation
▨ National Park Service
▨ National Forest land

0 ____ 50 miles
0 ____ 50 kilometers

N

North Carolina

 Land & Water Mount Mitchell, Lake Norman, and the Cape Fear River are important land and water features of North Carolina.

 Statehood North Carolina became the 12th state in 1789.

 People & Places North Carolina's population is 10,042,802. Raleigh is the state capital. The largest city is Charlotte.

Fun Fact The University of North Carolina, the first public university in the United States, opened its doors in 1795 with 2 professors and 41 students.

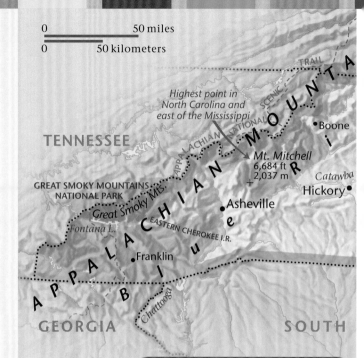

0 — 50 miles
0 — 50 kilometers

TRAIL
APPALACHIAN NATIONAL SCENIC
MOUNTA
TENNESSEE
Highest point in North Carolina and east of the Mississippi
•Boone
Mt. Mitchell
6,684 ft
2,037 m
i
Catawba
Hickory•
GREAT SMOKY MOUNTAINS NATIONAL PARK
Great Smoky Mts.
R
•Asheville
Fontana L.
EASTERN CHEROKEE I.R.
e
A
P
P
A
L
A
C
H
I
A
N
•Franklin
B
l
u
Chattooga
GEORGIA
SOUTH

North Carolina State Flag

N ★ C
MAY 20ᵗʰ 1775
APRIL 12ᵗʰ 1776

Cardinal
State Bird

Flowering Dogwood
State Flower

↑ The chapel tower is a landmark on the campus of Duke University in **Durham.**

← Basketball is a popular sport among all ages in **North Carolina,** whether on the court or in the backyard.

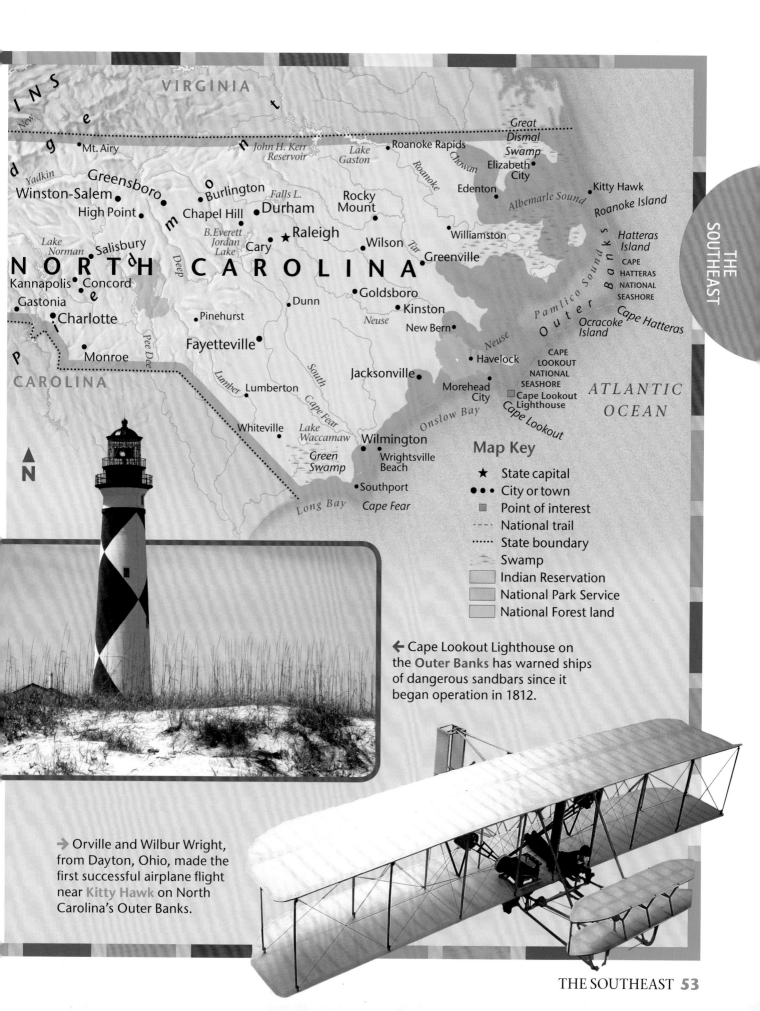

VIRGINIA

Great
Dismal
Swamp

INS

New

d
g
e

P
i
e
d
m
o
n
t

Yadkin

• Mt. Airy

John H. Kerr
Reservoir

Lake
Gaston

• Roanoke Rapids

Elizabeth •
City

Chowan

Roanoke

• Kitty Hawk

Greensboro

Burlington

Falls L.

Rocky
Mount

• Edenton

Albemarle Sound

Roanoke Island

Winston-Salem

Chapel Hill

Durham

High Point

B.Everett
Jordan
Lake

Cary

★ Raleigh

• Wilson

Williamston •

Hatteras
Island

CAPE
HATTERAS
NATIONAL
SEASHORE

Lake
Norman

Salisbury

Deep

Tar

• Greenville

Outer Banks

Pamlico Sounds

N O R T H   C A R O L I N A

Kannapolis

• Concord

Gastonia

• Charlotte

Pee Dee

Pinehurst

• Dunn

• Goldsboro

Neuse

• Kinston

Ocracoke
Island

Cape Hatteras

New Bern •

• Monroe

CAROLINA

Fayetteville •

South

Neuse

CAPE
LOOKOUT
NATIONAL
SEASHORE

ATLANTIC
OCEAN

Lumber

Jacksonville •

• Havelock

Lumberton •

Cape Fear

Morehead
City

□ Cape Lookout
Lighthouse

• Whiteville

Lake
Waccamaw

Wilmington •

Onslow Bay

Cape Lookout

Green
Swamp

Wrightsville
Beach

• Southport

Long Bay

Cape Fear

Map Key

★ State capital

••• City or town

□ Point of interest

--- National trail

····· State boundary

Swamp

Indian Reservation

National Park Service

National Forest land

← Cape Lookout Lighthouse on
the **Outer Banks** has warned ships
of dangerous sandbars since it
began operation in 1812.

→ Orville and Wilbur Wright,
from Dayton, Ohio, made the
first successful airplane flight
near **Kitty Hawk** on North
Carolina's Outer Banks.

N

SOUTH CAROLINA

South Carolina

Land & Water Sumter National Forest, Lake Marion, and the Great Pee Dee River are important land and water features of South Carolina.

Statehood South Carolina became the 8th state in 1788.

People & Places South Carolina's population is 4,896,146. Columbia is the state capital and the largest city.

Fun Fact Sweetgrass baskets have been made in the coastal lowland region for more than 300 years. They were originally used in the planting and processing of rice.

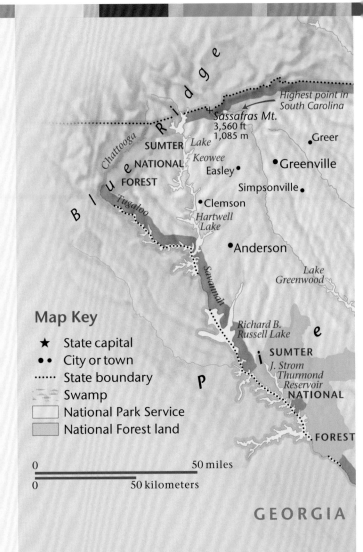

Highest point in South Carolina

Sassafras Mt.
3,560 ft
1,085 m

Chattooga

Blue Ridge

SUMTER

NATIONAL

FOREST

Tugaloo

Lake Keowee

Easley

Clemson

Hartwell Lake

Greer

Greenville

Simpsonville

Anderson

Lake Greenwood

Richard B. Russell Lake

Savannah

SUMTER

J. Strom Thurmond Reservoir

NATIONAL

FOREST

GEORGIA

Map Key

★ State capital
•• City or town
····· State boundary
~~ Swamp
☐ National Park Service
☐ National Forest land

0		50 miles
0		50 kilometers

↓ Large container ships carrying valuable manufactured goods link South Carolina to the global economy. **Charleston** is the state's largest port.

South Carolina State Flag

Yellow Jessamine
State Flower

Carolina Wren
State Bird

NORTH CAROLINA

KINGS MOUNTAIN
N.M.P.

Gaffney

Spartanburg

York

Rock Hill

Wylie Lake

Broad

Catawba

Lancaster

Cheraw

Union

SUMTER

Great Pee Dee

Dillon

↑ Loggerhead turtles, which are an endangered species, lay their eggs in nests that they dig in the sand of the coastal area known as the **Lowcountry.**

NATIONAL

FOREST

Winnsboro

Wateree
Lake

Wateree

Darlington

Florence

Newberry

Lake
Murray

Saluda

Irmo

SOUTH

Loris

Little Pee Dee

West Columbia

★ Columbia

Sumter

Lake City

Great Pee Dee

CAROLINA

CONGAREE
NATIONAL PARK

Congaree

Myrtle Beach

Aiken

S. Fork Edisto

N. Fork Edisto

Orangeburg

Black

Waccamaw

Long Bay

Williston

Lake
Marion

Georgetown

North
Island

ATLANTIC

Bamberg

Edisto

Lake
Moultrie

Santee

Cape Island

OCEAN

Savannah

Allendale

Moncks Corner

Cooper

Summerville

Walterboro

North
Charleston

Mount
Pleasant

Charleston

↓ Hard-packed sands on a **Hilton Head Island** beach are perfect for a family bicycle outing.

N

Coastal

Lowcountry

Edisto
Island

St. Helena
Sound

Beaufort

St. Helena
Island

Parris Island

Port Royal Sound

Hilton Head
Island

Hilton Head Island

Daufuskie Island

TENNESSEE

Tennessee

Land & Water The Cumberland Plateau, Reelfoot Lake, and the Tennessee River are important land and water features of Tennessee.

Statehood Tennessee became the 16th state in 1796.

People & Places Tennessee's population is 6,600,299. Nashville is the state capital. The largest city is Memphis.

Fun Fact In 1811–1812 three major earthquakes, known as the New Madrid earthquakes, changed the landscape in parts of Tennessee and Missouri. The ground in northwest Tennessee sank, creating Reelfoot Lake.

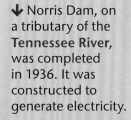

Tennessee State Flag

Iris
State Flower

Mockingbird
State Bird

MISSOURI

Kentucky Lake   Lake

Union City
Reelfoot L.   Martin   Paris
Obion
Dyersburg

ARKANSAS

Jackson

Bartlett
Germantown   Savannah
Memphis   Collierville   Pickwick Lake

Mississippi

Hatchie

Tennessee

MISSISSIPPI

➔ **Memphis** is famous for its barbecue, especially baby back ribs that are cooked so long that the meat falls from the bones.

⬇ Norris Dam, on a tributary of the **Tennessee River**, was completed in 1936. It was constructed to generate electricity.

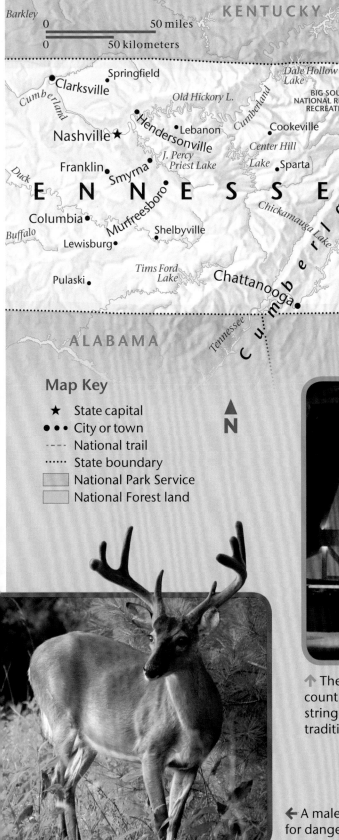

Map

KENTUCKY

VIRGINIA

Barkley

0   50 miles
0   50 kilometers

Cumberland

Springfield

Clarksville

Dale Hollow Lake

BIG SOUTH FORK NATIONAL RIVER AND RECREATION AREA

Old Hickory L.

Cookeville

Cumberland

CUMBERLAND GAP N.H.P.

Bristol

Kingsport

Johnson City

Norris Lake

Clinch

Nashville ★

Hendersonville

Lebanon

Center Hill Lake

Sparta

Knoxville

Morristown

Cherokee Lake

Oak Ridge

Douglas Lake

Newport

Sevierville

French Broad

Nolichucky

Franklin

Smyrna

J. Percy Priest Lake

Fort Loudoun Lake

Gatlinburg

Great Smoky Mts.

APPALACHIAN

SCENIC

TRAIL

T E N N E S S E E

Duck

Watts Bar Lake

Maryville

Clingmans Dome 6,643 ft 2,025 m

NORTH CAROLINA

Columbia

Murfreesboro

Shelbyville

Chickamauga Lake

Tellico Lake

Tennessee

Athens

GREAT SMOKY MOUNTAINS NATIONAL PARK

Highest point in Tennessee

Buffalo

Lewisburg

Tims Ford Lake

Chattanooga

Cleveland

Hiwassee

Pulaski

Tennessee

SOUTH CAROLINA

ALABAMA

Cumberland Plateau

Appalachian Mountains

GEORGIA

Map Key

★   State capital
•••   City or town
---   National trail
····   State boundary
▢   National Park Service
▢   National Forest land

N

⬆ The Grand Ole Opry in **Nashville** is the home of country music. Country music performers mainly use stringed instruments. This music form evolved from traditional folk tunes of the Appalachians.

⬅ A male white-tailed deer with a full rack of antlers watches for danger in a meadow in **Great Smoky Mountains National Park.** The park is a popular vacation destination.

VIRGINIA

The Southeast

Virginia

Land & Water
The Blue Ridge mountains, Shenandoah National Park, and the James River are important land and water features of Virginia.

Statehood
Virginia became the 10th state in 1788.

People & Places
Virginia's population is 8,382,993. Richmond is the state capital. The largest city is Virginia Beach.

Fun Fact
Eight U.S. presidents—Washington, Jefferson, Madison, Monroe, Harrison, Tyler, Taylor, and Wilson—were born in Virginia, more than in any other state.

↑ An old barn, bales of hay, and trees in autumn foliage are a common sight in the **Appalachian Mountains** of Virginia.

↓ A fife and drum band maintains the tradition of military music as it marches down a street in **Williamsburg,** an early capital of Virginia.

Virginia State Flag

Flowering Dogwood
State Flower

Cardinal
State Bird

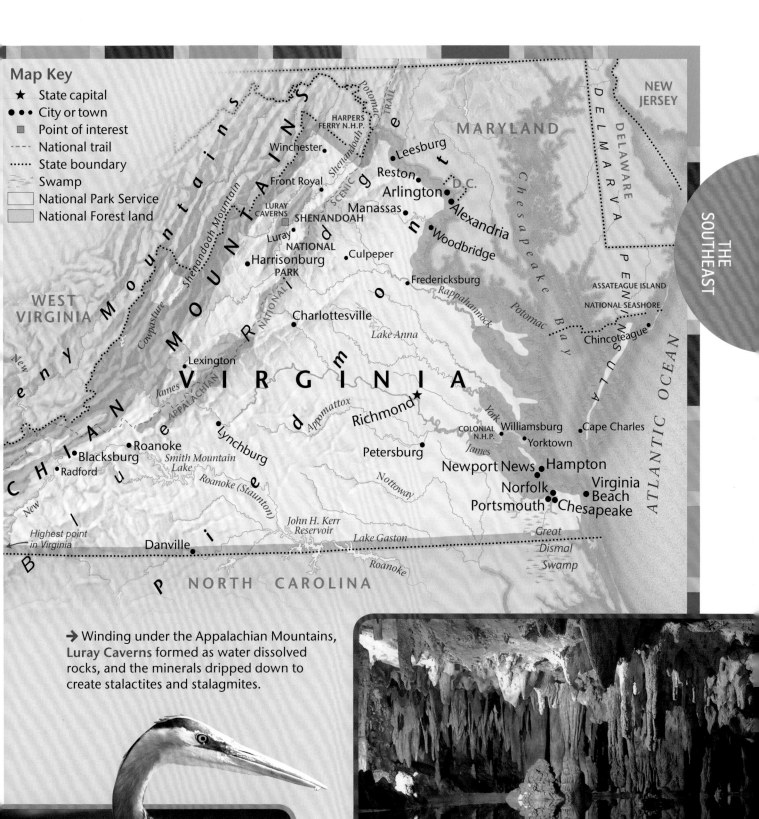

Map Key

★ State capital
● ● ● City or town
▪ Point of interest
--- National trail
⋯⋯ State boundary
〰 Swamp
☐ National Park Service
☐ National Forest land

WEST VIRGINIA

Allegheny Mountains

New

Blue Ridge Mountains

APPALACHIAN NATIONAL SCENIC TRAIL

Shenandoah Mountain

Shenandoah Mountains

Shenandoah

HARPERS FERRY N.H.P.

Winchester

Front Royal

LURAY CAVERNS

Luray

SHENANDOAH NATIONAL PARK

Harrisonburg

Highest point in Virginia

Lexington

Blacksburg
Radford
Roanoke

New

Cowpasture

James

Smith Mountain Lake

Lynchburg

Roanoke (Staunton)

VIRGINIA

Charlottesville

Culpeper

Lake Anna

Appomattox

Richmond ★

Petersburg

Nottoway

John H. Kerr Reservoir

Danville

Lake Gaston

Roanoke

POTOMAC HERITAGE TRAIL

Leesburg

Reston

Arlington

D.C.

Manassas

Woodbridge

Fredericksburg

Rappahannock

Potomac

MARYLAND

Chesapeake Bay

DELMARVA PENINSULA

DELAWARE

NEW JERSEY

ASSATEAGUE ISLAND NATIONAL SEASHORE

Chincoteague

Alexandria

York

COLONIAL N.H.P.

Williamsburg

Yorktown

James

Cape Charles

Newport News
Hampton
Norfolk
Virginia Beach
Portsmouth
Chesapeake

Great Dismal Swamp

ATLANTIC OCEAN

NORTH CAROLINA

→ Winding under the Appalachian Mountains, **Luray Caverns** formed as water dissolved rocks, and the minerals dripped down to create stalactites and stalagmites.

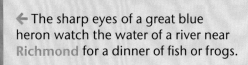

← The sharp eyes of a great blue heron watch the water of a river near **Richmond** for a dinner of fish or frogs.

West Virginia

Land & Water
The Allegheny Mountains, Ohio River, and the New River are important land and water features of West Virginia.

Statehood
West Virginia became the 35th state in 1863.

People & Places
West Virginia's population is 1,844,128. Charleston is the state capital and the largest city.

Fun Fact
One of the oldest and largest Indian burial grounds is located in Moundsville along the Ohio River. It is more than 2,000 years old and 69 feet (21 m) high.

↑ West Virginia's rivers offer some of the best white-water rafting in the eastern United States. The **Gauley River** is called the Beast of the East.

← A coal miner's helmet recalls the history of mining in **West Virginia**. The state produced almost 12 percent of U.S. coal in 2012.

↓ Trees turn red in the **Dolly Sods Wilderness** in the Monongahela National Forest. The area is named for an early settler family.

West Virginia State Flag

Rhododendron
State Flower

Cardinal
State Bird

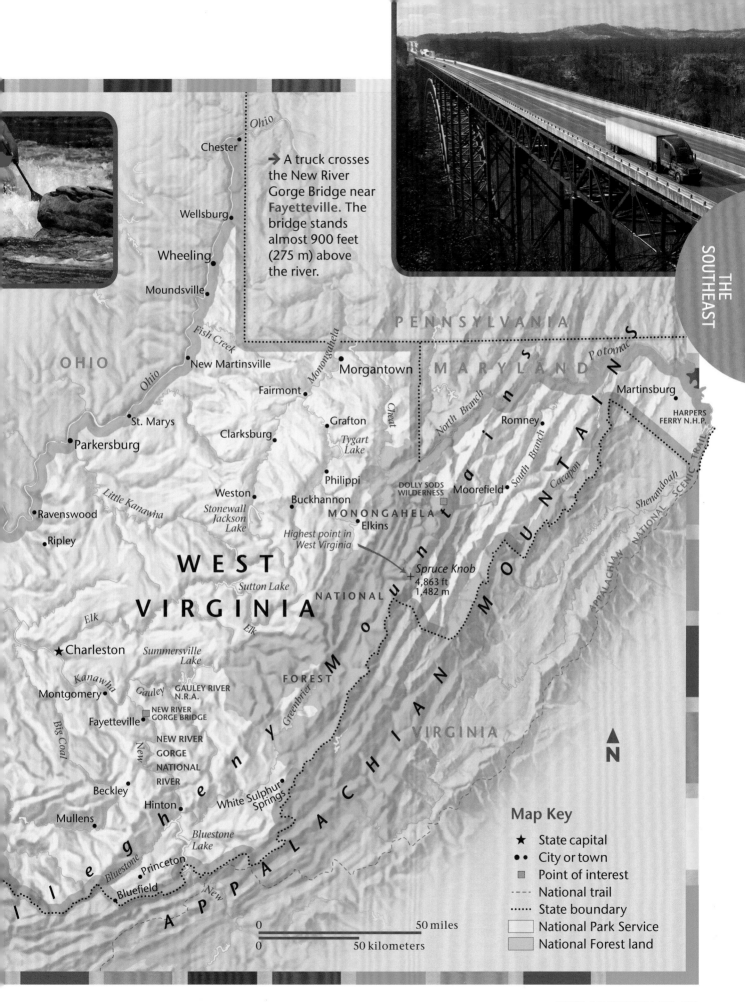

→ A truck crosses the New River Gorge Bridge near **Fayetteville**. The bridge stands almost 900 feet (275 m) above the river.

PENNSYLVANIA

OHIO

Ohio

Chester

Wellsburg

Wheeling

Moundsville

Fish Creek

New Martinsville

Ohio

St. Marys

Parkersburg

Ravenswood

Ripley

Little Kanawha

WEST VIRGINIA

Elk

Elk

★ Charleston

Kanawha

Montgomery

Gauley

GAULEY RIVER N.R.A.

Big Coal

Fayetteville

NEW RIVER GORGE BRIDGE

New

NEW RIVER GORGE NATIONAL RIVER

Beckley

Mullens

Hinton

Bluestone

Bluestone Lake

Princeton

Bluefield

New

Fairmont

Morgantown

Monongahela

Cheat

Grafton

Clarksburg

Tygart Lake

Philippi

Buckhannon

Weston

Stonewall Jackson Lake

MONONGAHELA

Elkins

Highest point in West Virginia

Sutton Lake

NATIONAL

FOREST

Greenbrier

Summersville Lake

White Sulphur Springs

MARYLAND

Potomac

North Branch

South Branch

Cacapon

Romney

Moorefield

DOLLY SODS WILDERNESS

+ Spruce Knob
4,863 ft
1,482 m

Martinsburg

HARPERS FERRY N.H.P.

Shenandoah

APPALACHIAN NATIONAL SCENIC TRAIL

VIRGINIA

Allegheny Mountains

APPALACHIAN MOUNTAINS

N

Map Key

★ State capital
•• City or town
■ Point of interest
--- National trail
•••• State boundary
☐ National Park Service
☐ National Forest land

0   50 miles
0   50 kilometers

The Midwest

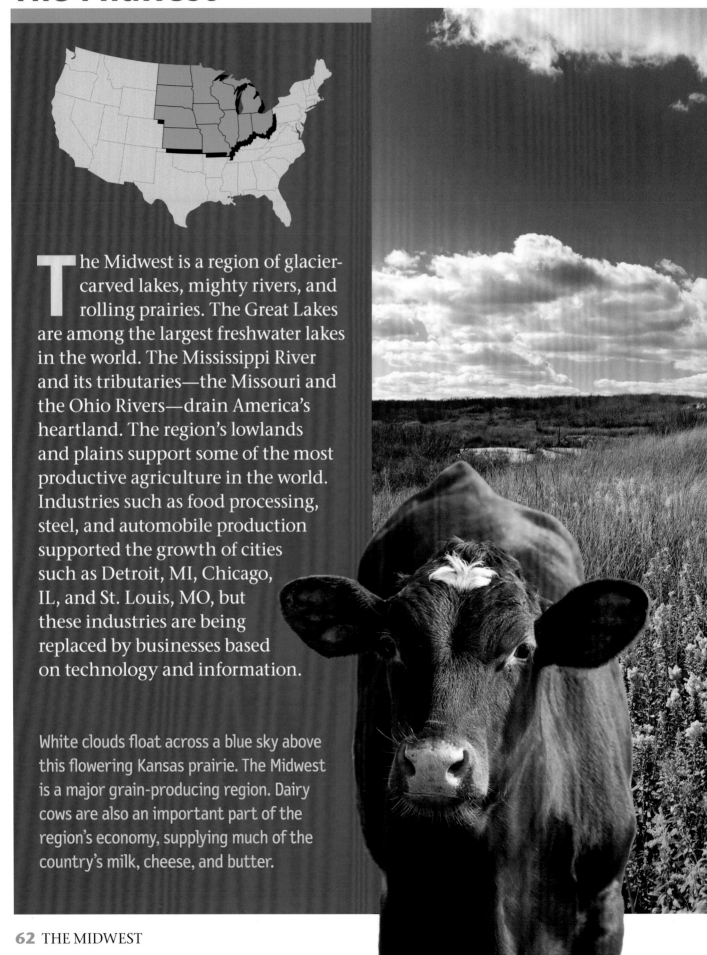

The Midwest is a region of glacier-carved lakes, mighty rivers, and rolling prairies. The Great Lakes are among the largest freshwater lakes in the world. The Mississippi River and its tributaries—the Missouri and the Ohio Rivers—drain America's heartland. The region's lowlands and plains support some of the most productive agriculture in the world. Industries such as food processing, steel, and automobile production supported the growth of cities such as Detroit, MI, Chicago, IL, and St. Louis, MO, but these industries are being replaced by businesses based on technology and information.

White clouds float across a blue sky above this flowering Kansas prairie. The Midwest is a major grain-producing region. Dairy cows are also an important part of the region's economy, supplying much of the country's milk, cheese, and butter.

ILLINOIS

Illinois

Land & Water
The Shawnee National Forest, the Illinois River, and Lake Michigan are important land and water features of Illinois.

← Children ride bicycles along a sidewalk in Pilsen, on Chicago's lower west side. A street mural celebrates the neighborhood's immigrant roots.

Statehood
Illinois became the 21st state in 1818.

People & Places
Illinois has a population of 12,859,995. Springfield is the state capital. The largest city is Chicago.

Fun Fact
A river that runs through Chicago is dyed green on St. Patrick's Day to honor the city's large Irish population. The formula for the green dye is a closely kept secret.

↑ Pig races are a fun-filled highlight of the annual Illinois State Fair in Springfield.

ILLINOIS

Illinois State Flag

Violet
State Flower

Cardinal
State Bird

WRIGLEY FIELD HOME OF CHICAGO CUBS

PIRATES 1   TOP 9TH   CUBS 4

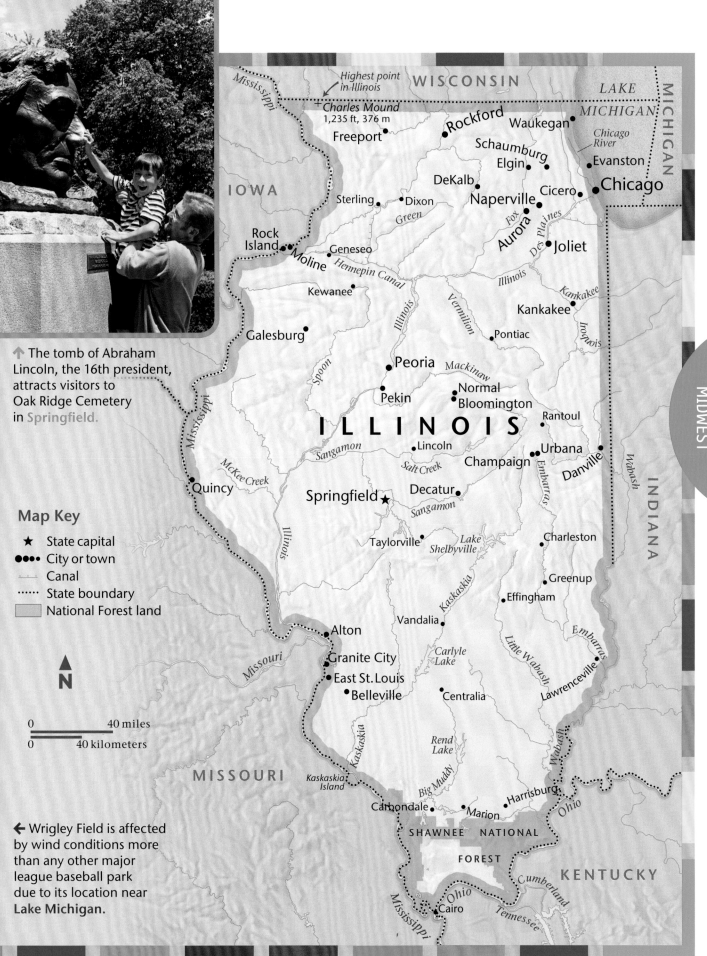

The tomb of Abraham Lincoln, the 16th president, attracts visitors to Oak Ridge Cemetery in Springfield.

Map Key

★ State capital
●●●● City or town
⊢—⊣ Canal
····· State boundary
⬜ National Forest land

↑
N

0 — 40 miles
0 — 40 kilometers

← Wrigley Field is affected by wind conditions more than any other major league baseball park due to its location near Lake Michigan.

WISCONSIN

LAKE MICHIGAN

Mississippi

Highest point in Illinois
⊹ Charles Mound
1,235 ft, 376 m

Freeport

Rockford   Waukegan

Chicago River

Schaumburg
Elgin   Evanston

DeKalb   Cicero   Chicago

IOWA

Sterling   Dixon   Naperville
Green

Rock Island   Geneseo   Aurora   Joliet

Moline   Hennepin Canal   Fox   Des Plaines

Kewanee   Illinois

Kankakee

Galesburg   Vermilion   Kankakee

Illinois   Pontiac   Iroquois

Spoon   Peoria   Mackinaw

Pekin   Normal
Bloomington

ILLINOIS   Rantoul

Sangamon   Lincoln   Urbana

Salt Creek   Champaign   Embarras   Danville

McKee Creek   Springfield ★   Decatur

Quincy   Sangamon

Taylorville   Lake Shelbyville   Charleston

Illinois   Kaskaskia   Greenup

Effingham

Little Wabash   Embarras

Vandalia   Lawrenceville

Alton   Carlyle Lake

Missouri   Granite City
East St. Louis   Centralia
Belleville

Kaskaskia   Rend Lake   Big Muddy   Wabash

MISSOURI

Kaskaskia Island   Harrisburg
Carbondale   Marion   Ohio
Cumberland

SHAWNEE   NATIONAL

FOREST   KENTUCKY

Mississippi   Ohio
Cairo   Tennessee

INDIANA

Wabash

INDIANA

Indiana

 Land & Water The Hoosier National Forest, Lake Michigan, and the Wabash River are important land and water features of Indiana.

 Statehood Indiana became the 19th state in 1816.

 People & Places Indiana's population is 6,619,680. Indianapolis is the state capital and the largest city.

 Fun Fact The intersection of U.S. Highway 40 and U.S. Highway 41, at Wabash Avenue and Seventh Street in Terre Haute, is called the Crossroads of America.

↑ The **Indianapolis** Motor Speedway is the largest sports stadium in the world. It seats 250,000 and hosts the famous Indy 500.

→ The Hoosiers of Indiana University, located in **Bloomington**, are a part of college football's powerful Big Ten Conference. Sports are an important tradition and a favorite pastime in Indiana.

Indiana State Flag

Peony
State Flower

Cardinal
State Bird

Map Key

★ State capital
••• City or town
•••• State boundary
State Park
National Park Service
National Forest land

0 _____ 100 miles
0 _____ 100 kilometers

N

⬇ A boy gathers sweet corn on a family farm near **Centerville**. Corn is an important food for both people and livestock.

LAKE MICHIGAN

MICHIGAN

East Chicago
Hammond
Gary
Merrillville
Portage
Valparaiso

Michigan City
INDIANA DUNES NAT. LAKESHORE
South Bend
Mishawaka
Elkhart
Goshen
Angola

Plymouth
Auburn

Warsaw

Kankakee

Tippecanoe

Fort Wayne

St. Joseph
Maumee
St. Marys

Rensselaer

Eel

Huntington

Iroquois

Wabash

Wabash

Mississinewa Lake

Kokomo
Marion

OHIO

Lafayette

I N D I A N A

Muncie

Highest point in Indiana
White
Hoosier Hill
1,257 ft
383 m

Lebanon
Noblesville
Anderson

Carmel

Sugar Creek

New Castle
Richmond
Centerville

Sugar Creek

Indianapolis ★
Lawrence

Plainfield
Beech Grove

Connersville

Greenwood

Big Blue

Shelbyville

Brookville Lake

Terre Haute

Cagles Mill Lake

Mill Creek

White

Franklin

Martinsville

Lake Lemon

Columbus

BROWN COUNTY STATE PARK

Sand Creek

Lawrenceburg

Bloomington

Monroe Lake

HOOSIER

Bedford

Muscatatuck

Whitewater

Great Miami

Eel

Wabash

Salt Cr.

Ohio

Vincennes
Washington

East Fork White

NATIONAL

Blue

Jeffersonville

Ohio

White

Patoka

Patoka Lake

New Albany

FOREST

KENTUCKY

Mount Vernon
Evansville

Ohio

IOWA

Iowa

Land & Water
Hawkeye Point and the Missouri and Mississippi Rivers are important land and water features of Iowa.

Statehood Iowa became the 29th state in 1846.

People & Places Iowa's population is 3,123,899. Des Moines is the state capital and the largest city.

Fun Fact Iowa's nickname, the Hawkeye State, comes from Chief Black Hawk, the Sauk Indian chief who started the Black Hawk War in 1832.

↑ Hogs outnumber people almost seven to one in Iowa, which produces nearly one-third of all hogs raised in the United States.

Hawkeye Point +
1,670 ft
509 m

Highest point in Iowa

SOUTH DAKOTA

Big Sioux

• Sheldon

Le Mars •

• Sioux City

Missouri

Little Sioux

• Onawa

Denison •

Boyer

NEBRASKA

Harlan •

• Council Bluffs

• Glenwood

Missouri

Map Key

★ State capital
••• City or town
▪ Point of interest
······ State boundary

Iowa State Flag

IOWA

OUR LIBERTIES WE PRIZE AND OUR RIGHTS WE WILL MAINTAIN

Wild Rose
State Flower

American Goldfinch
State Bird

← A young Native American boy dressed in colorful traditional clothing prepares to participate in the Annual Meskwaki Powwow near Tama.

MINNESOTA

WISCONSIN

Forest City
Osage
Wapsipinicon
New Hampton
Effigy Mounds Nat. Mon.

Spencer
Emmetsburg
Charles City
Shell Rock
Cedar
Marquette

Des Moines
Mason City
Iowa
Waverly
Oelwein
Turkey

Storm Lake
Humboldt
Cedar Falls
Waterloo
Manchester
Dubuque

Fort Dodge
Webster City
Monticello

Raccoon
Maquoketa

I O W A

Jefferson
Ames
Tama
Cedar Rapids
Clinton

Perry
Marshalltown
Cedar
Bettendorf

Ankeny
Newton
Iowa City
Davenport

Urbandale
★ Des Moines
Iowa

West Des Moines
Pella

Atlantic
Indianola
Lake Red Rock
Washington

Thompson
Oskaloosa

Red Oak
Ottumwa
Mount Pleasant

ILLINOIS

Chariton
Rathbun Lake

Clarinda
Bloomfield
Burlington

Centerville
Des Moines

MISSOURI
Mississippi
Keokuk

N

| 0 | | 50 miles |
| 0 | | 50 kilometers |

→ Effigy Mounds National Monument, near Marquette, preserves 206 sacred mounds created by American Indians more than 1,000 years ago.

← Paper-thin sheets of 23-karat gold cover the central dome of Iowa's state capitol building in Des Moines.

EFFIGY MOUNDS

NATIONAL MONUMENT

Headquarters-Visitor Center-Museum →

KANSAS

The Midwest

Kansas

 Land & Water Mount Sunflower, the Flint Hills, and the Missouri River are important land and water features of Kansas.

 Statehood Kansas became the 34th state in 1861.

 People & Places The population of Kansas is 2,911,641. Topeka is the state capital. The largest city is Wichita.

 Fun Fact Pizza Hut, the world's largest pizza chain, opened its first restaurant in Wichita in 1958. Today the company has branches in more than 100 countries.

Kansas State Flag

Sunflower
State Flower

Western Meadowlark
State Bird

↑ A statue of the Tin Man, a character from *The Wonderful Wizard of Oz*, the popular fantasy book partly set in Kansas, sits in a garden.

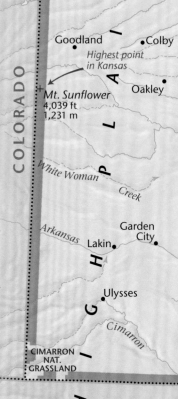

Goodland •Colby
Highest point in Kansas
+ Mt. Sunflower Oakley
4,039 ft
1,231 m
White Woman Creek
Arkansas Lakin• Garden City•
Ulysses
Cimarron
CIMARRON NAT. GRASSLAND
COLORADO
HIGH PLAINS

Map Key

★ State capital
••• City or town
····· State boundary
◻ Indian Reservation
◻ National Park Service
◻ National Grassland

↓ Monument Rocks, located south of Oakley, were once part of an ancient inland sea bed. Over millions of years, erosion by wind and water has created these chalk formations.

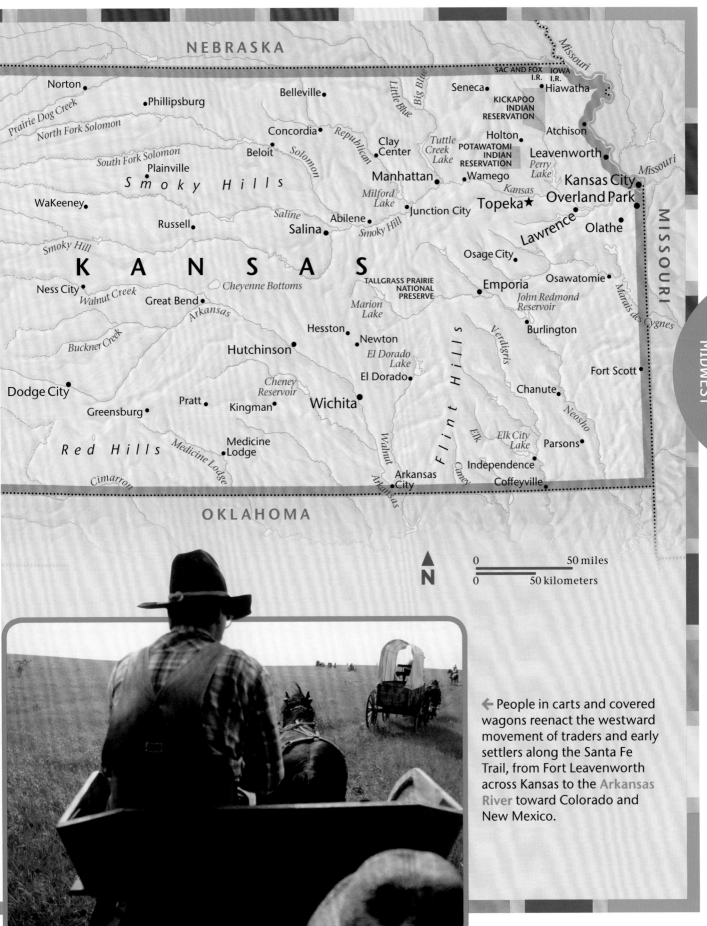

NEBRASKA

Norton
Phillipsburg
Belleville
Prairie Dog Creek
North Fork Solomon
Concordia
Little Blue
Big Blue
Seneca
SAC AND FOX I.R.
IOWA I.R.
Hiawatha
KICKAPOO INDIAN RESERVATION
Atchison
Missouri

Beloit
Republican
Clay Center
Holton
POTAWATOMI INDIAN RESERVATION
Leavenworth
South Fork Solomon
Plainville
Solomon
Tuttle Creek Lake
Perry Lake

Smoky Hills
Manhattan
Wamego
Kansas
Kansas City
Overland Park
Missouri

WaKeeney
Milford Lake
Topeka ★

Russell
Saline
Abilene
Junction City
Lawrence
Olathe

Salina
Smoky Hill
MISSOURI

Smoky Hill

K A N S A S
Osage City

Cheyenne Bottoms
TALLGRASS PRAIRIE NATIONAL PRESERVE
Emporia
Osawatomie

Ness City
Walnut Creek
Great Bend
Marion Lake
John Redmond Reservoir
Marais des Cygnes

Arkansas
Hesston
Newton
Burlington

Buckner Creek
Hutchinson
El Dorado Lake
Verdigris

Dodge City
Cheney Reservoir
El Dorado
Flint Hills
Chanute
Fort Scott

Greensburg
Pratt
Kingman
Wichita
Neosho

Red Hills
Medicine Lodge
Walnut
Elk
Elk City Lake
Parsons

Cimarron
Medicine Lodge
Arkansas City
Independence
Coffeyville

Arkansas
Caney

OKLAHOMA

N

| 0 | 50 miles |
| 0 | 50 kilometers |

THE MIDWEST

← People in carts and covered wagons reenact the westward movement of traders and early settlers along the Santa Fe Trail, from Fort Leavenworth across Kansas to the Arkansas River toward Colorado and New Mexico.

Michigan

Land & Water The Upper and Lower Peninsulas and Lakes Superior, Michigan, and Huron are important land and water features of Michigan.

Statehood Michigan became the 26th state in 1837.

People & Places Michigan's population is 9,922,576. Lansing is the state capital. The largest city is Detroit.

Fun Fact The record company Motown, named for Detroit's nickname Motor City, grew from a small start-up business in 1959 to one of the largest independent record companies in the world.

← A statue of Austin Blair, governor of Michigan during the Civil War, stands in front of the state capitol in Lansing.

← Boys explore nature's wonders on the bank of a river near Niles. The town sits on the site of Fort St. Joseph, built by the French in 1691.

↓ The Straits of Mackinac join Lakes Michigan and Huron. Crossing the straits, the five-mile (8-km)-long Mackinac Bridge connects Michigan's Upper Peninsula to the southern part of the state.

Michigan State Flag

Apple Blossom
State Flower

Robin
State Bird

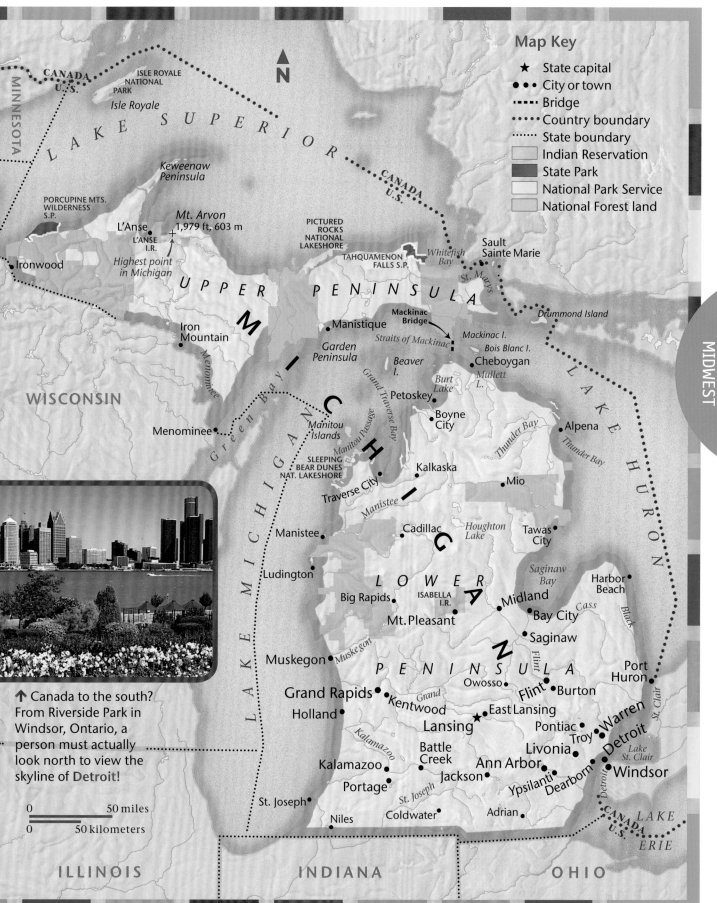

Map Key

★ State capital
●●● City or town
┅┅ Bridge
•••• Country boundary
···· State boundary
▢ Indian Reservation
▢ State Park
▢ National Park Service
▢ National Forest land

MINNESOTA

CANADA
U.S.

ISLE ROYALE NATIONAL PARK

Isle Royale

LAKE SUPERIOR

CANADA
U.S.

Keweenaw Peninsula

PORCUPINE MTS. WILDERNESS S.P.

L'Anse
L'ANSE I.R.

Mt. Arvon
1,979 ft, 603 m

Highest point in Michigan

Ironwood

PICTURED ROCKS NATIONAL LAKESHORE

TAHQUAMENON FALLS S.P.

Whitefish Bay

Sault Sainte Marie

St. Marys

UPPER PENINSULA

M

Iron Mountain

Manistique

Garden Peninsula

Mackinac Bridge

Straits of Mackinac

Mackinac I.

Bois Blanc I.

Drummond Island

Cheboygan

Mullett L.

WISCONSIN

I

Beaver I.

Burt Lake

Petoskey

Boyne City

LAKE HURON

Menominee

Menominee

Green Bay

Manitou Islands

Manitou Passage

C

Grand Traverse Bay

Alpena

Thunder Bay

Thunder Bay

SLEEPING BEAR DUNES NAT. LAKESHORE

H

Kalkaska

Mio

Traverse City

Manistee

Manistee

I

Cadillac

Houghton Lake

Tawas City

Ludington

G

LOWER

Saginaw Bay

Harbor Beach

Big Rapids

ISABELLA I.R.

A

Midland

Cass

Mt. Pleasant

Bay City

Saginaw

Muskegon

Muskegon

N

Flint

Black

PENINSULA

Owosso

Flint

Burton

Port Huron

Grand Rapids

Kentwood

Grand

East Lansing

St. Clair

Holland

Lansing ★

Pontiac

Troy

Warren

Livonia

Detroit

Kalamazoo

Battle Creek

Ann Arbor

Dearborn

Lake St. Clair

Portage

Jackson

Ypsilanti

Windsor

St. Joseph

St. Joseph

Detroit

CANADA
U.S.

LAKE ERIE

Niles

Coldwater

Adrian

ILLINOIS

INDIANA

OHIO

↑ Canada to the south? From Riverside Park in Windsor, Ontario, a person must actually look north to view the skyline of **Detroit**!

0 ——— 50 miles
0 ——— 50 kilometers

Minnesota

← Minnesota's gray wolf population is growing and no longer endangered thanks to the work of the International Wolf Center in Ely.

 Land & Water Chippewa National Forest, Lake Superior, and the Mississippi River are important land and water features of Minnesota.

 Statehood Minnesota became the 32nd state in 1858.

 People & Places Minnesota's population is 5,489,594. St. Paul is the state capital. The largest city is Minneapolis.

 Fun Fact Modern in-line skates were invented by two Minnesota students. Looking for a way to practice hockey in the summer, they replaced their skate blades with wheels.

↓ Some people in Minnesota sit for hours in "ice shacks" and fish through holes cut in the ice of frozen lakes.

Minnesota State Flag

Showy Lady's Slipper
State Flower

Common Loon
State Bird

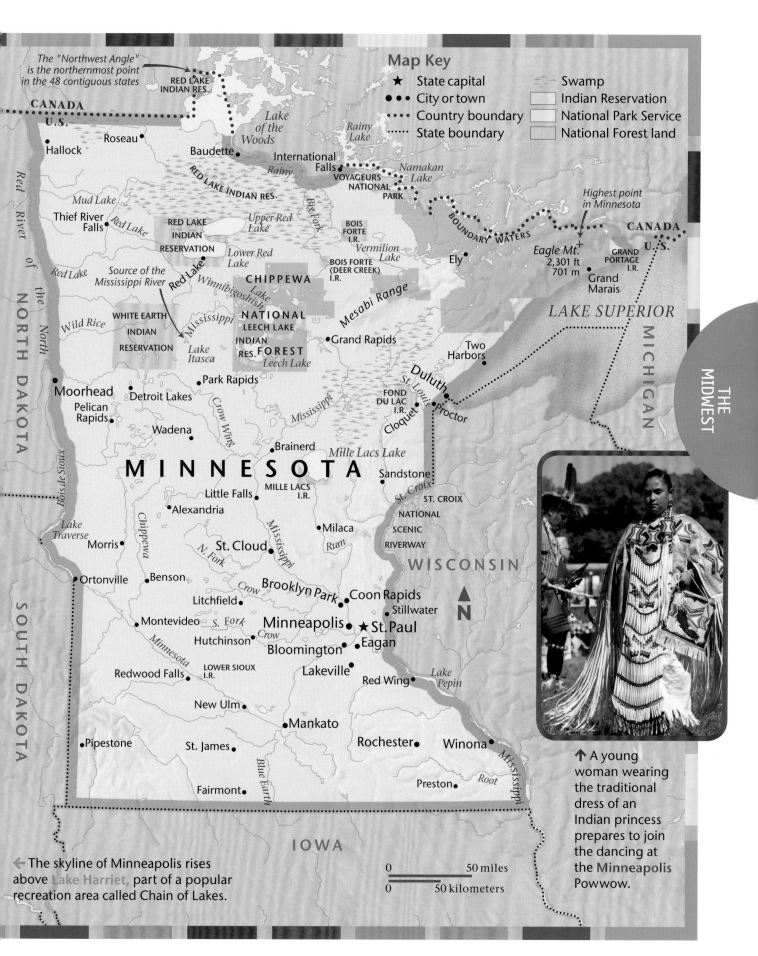

Map Key

★ State capital	∼ Swamp
● ● ● City or town	▢ Indian Reservation
···· Country boundary	▢ National Park Service
····· State boundary	▢ National Forest land

The "Northwest Angle" is the northernmost point in the 48 contiguous states

RED LAKE INDIAN RES.

Lake of the Woods

Rainy Lake

CANADA
U.S.

Roseau

Hallock

Baudette

International Falls

Rainy

VOYAGEURS NATIONAL PARK

Namakan Lake

Mud Lake

RED LAKE INDIAN RES.

Big Fork

BOIS FORTE I.R.

Vermilion Lake

BOIS FORTE (DEER CREEK) I.R.

BOUNDARY WATERS

Highest point in Minnesota

Eagle Mt. 2,301 ft 701 m

CANADA
U.S.

GRAND PORTAGE I.R.

Thief River Falls

Red Lake

Upper Red Lake

RED LAKE INDIAN RESERVATION

Lower Red Lake

Ely

Grand Marais

Red River

of

the

North

NORTH DAKOTA

Source of the Mississippi River

Red Lake

Winnibigoshish

Lake

CHIPPEWA

Mesabi Range

LAKE SUPERIOR

MICHIGAN

Wild Rice

WHITE EARTH INDIAN RESERVATION

Mississippi

Lake Itasca

NATIONAL

LEECH LAKE INDIAN RES.

FOREST

Leech Lake

Grand Rapids

Two Harbors

THE MIDWEST

Moorhead

Detroit Lakes

Park Rapids

Crow Wing

Mississippi

Duluth

FOND DU LAC I.R.

St. Louis

Proctor

Pelican Rapids

Wadena

Cloquet

Bois de Sioux

Brainerd

Mille Lacs Lake

Sandstone

St. Croix

MINNESOTA

MILLE LACS I.R.

ST. CROIX NATIONAL SCENIC RIVERWAY

Little Falls

Lake Traverse

Alexandria

Milaca

Rum

Mississippi

WISCONSIN

N

Morris

Chippewa

N. Fork

St. Cloud

Ortonville

Benson

Crow

Brooklyn Park

Coon Rapids

Litchfield

Stillwater

Montevideo

S. Fork

Minneapolis

★ St. Paul

SOUTH DAKOTA

Hutchinson

Crow

Bloomington

Eagan

Minnesota

LOWER SIOUX I.R.

Lakeville

Redwood Falls

Red Wing

Lake Pepin

New Ulm

Mankato

Pipestone

St. James

Rochester

Winona

Blue Earth

Preston

Root

Mississippi

Fairmont

IOWA

← The skyline of Minneapolis rises above Lake Harriet, part of a popular recreation area called Chain of Lakes.

↑ A young woman wearing the traditional dress of an Indian princess prepares to join the dancing at the Minneapolis Powwow.

0		50 miles
0		50 kilometers

MISSOURI

Missouri

Land & Water Mark Twain National Forest and the Missouri and Mississippi Rivers are important land and water features of Missouri.

Statehood Missouri became the 24th state in 1821.

People & Places Missouri's population is 6,083,672. Jefferson City is the state capital. The largest city is Kansas City.

Fun Fact Mark Twain's childhood in Hannibal, a town on the Mississippi River, inspired many of his books, including *The Adventures of Tom Sawyer* and *The Adventures of Huckleberry Finn*.

Missouri State Flag

Eastern Bluebird
State Bird

Hawthorn
State Flower

↑ In 2004 St. Charles celebrated the bicentennial of the Lewis and Clark expedition, which explored the northwestern part of the Louisiana Purchase. The historic journey began in Missouri.

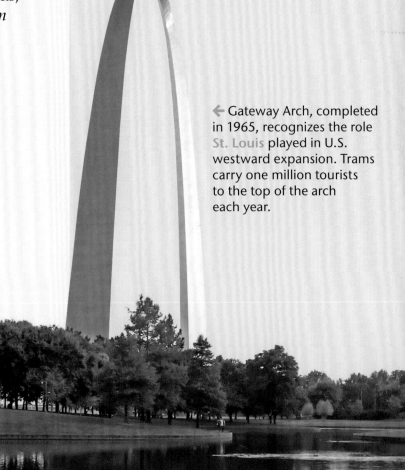

← Gateway Arch, completed in 1965, recognizes the role St. Louis played in U.S. westward expansion. Trams carry one million tourists to the top of the arch each year.

IOWA

Missouri

NEBR.

Maryville

Bethany

Thompson

Grand

Trenton

Chillicothe

Chariton

Middle Fabius

South Fabius

Mississippi

0   50 miles
0   50 kilometers

N

Map Key

★ State capital
••• City or town
••••• State boundary
National Park Service
National Forest land

Platte

St. Joseph

Liberty

Kansas City

Independence

Blue Springs

Lees Summit

Blackwater

Marshall

Sedalia

Jefferson City ★

Columbia

MARK TWAIN
NATIONAL
FOREST

Fulton

Missouri

Hannibal

Salt

Moberly

Mark Twain
Lake

St. Charles

St. Peters

Florissant

University City

St. Louis

Kirkwood

ILLINOIS

M I S S O U R I

Harry S. Truman
Reservoir

Osage

Nevada

Lake of
the Ozarks

Osage

Gasconade

Sullivan

De Soto

Rolla

Highest point
in Missouri

Taum Sauk Mt.
1,772 ft, 540 m

Farmington

Mississippi

KANSAS

Stockton
Lake

Sac

Little Sac

Lebanon

Osage Fork

MARK TWAIN

Salem

NATIONAL

FOREST

Springfield

Joplin

Ava

OZARK
NATIONAL
SCENIC RIVERWAYS

Current

Cape Girardeau

Ohio

KENTUCKY

Eleven Point

Sikeston

P   L   A   T   E   A   U

MARK   TWAIN   NATIONAL   FOREST

Table Rock Lake

Branson

Black

Mississippi

O   Z

Bull Shoals Lake

Kennett

TENNESSEE

OKLAHOMA

A R K A N S A S

← A cannon stands
as a silent reminder
of battles fought in
Missouri during the
Civil War. Missouri
was a Border State—
a slave state that
stayed in the Union.

← White-tailed deer live
throughout Missouri, but
are most abundant in hills
along the Missouri River.

Nebraska

Land & Water
The Sand Hills and the Platte and Missouri Rivers are important land and water features of Nebraska.

Statehood
Nebraska became the 37th state in 1867.

People & Places
Nebraska's population is 1,896,190. Lincoln is the state capital. The largest city is Omaha.

Fun Fact
The largest remaining area of original native prairie in the United States is in the Sand Hills region. It is an important stopover for migrating sandhill cranes.

← Two black-tailed prairie dogs watch for signs of danger at the entrance to their burrow in the **Fort Niobrara National Wildlife Refuge.**

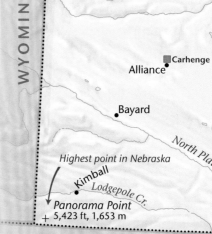

WYOMING

OGLALA NATIONAL GRASSLAND

Crawford • White Pine Ridge • Gordon

S a n d

P L A I N S

■ Carhenge
Alliance •

• Bayard

North Platte

Lake C.W. McConaughy

Highest point in Nebraska
• Kimball
Lodgepole Cr.
Panorama Point
+ 5,423 ft, 1,653 m

South Platte • Ogallala

COLORADO

H I G H

• Grant

• Imperial

Frenchman Cr.

↓ Tourists dressed like Indians and pioneers participate in a reenactment of a 19th-century wagon train under attack along the historic Oregon Trail near Bayard.

Nebraska State Flag

Goldenrod
State Flower

Western Meadowlark
State Bird

Map Key

★ State capital

●●● City or town

■ Point of interest

····· State boundary

Indian Reservation

National Forest land

National Grassland

National Wildlife Reserve

SOUTH DAKOTA

Valentine
Niobrara
FORT NIOBRARA N.W.R.

Gordon Cr.

Niobrara

Missouri

Lewis and Clark Lake

SANTEE INDIAN RES.

Hartington

Atkinson

Logan Creek

South Sioux City

WINNEBAGO I.R.

OMAHA I.R.

IOWA

H i l l s

Mullen

North Loup

Middle Loup

Elkhorn

Norfolk

Tekamah

E B R A S K A

Burwell

Broken Bow

Columbus

Fremont

Omaha

South Loup

Loup

Wahoo

Bellevue

North Platte

St. Paul

Big Blue

Platte

Plattsmouth

Platte

Gothenburg

Ravenna

Grand Island

York

★ Lincoln

Red Willow Creek

Kearney

Crete

Nebraska City

MISSOURI

Holdrege

Minden

Hastings

Geneva

Auburn

Missouri

Big Nemaha

McCook

Republican

Alma

Red Cloud

Superior

Little Blue

Fairbury

SAC AND FOX I.R.

IOWA I.R.

KANSAS

↑ In recent years annual snowfall in **Lincoln** has averaged about 25 inches (64 cm), creating work for adults but fun for kids.

0 ——— 50 miles
0 ——— 50 kilometers

N

→ Carhenge, near **Alliance**, is a sculpture made out of old cars that are painted gray and designed to look like Stonehenge, which is a famous archaeological site in southern England.

The Midwest

North Dakota

 Land & Water The Badlands, the Red River of the North, and the Missouri River are important land and water features of North Dakota.

Statehood North Dakota became the 39th state in 1889.

 People & Places North Dakota's population is 756,927. Bismarck is the state capital. The largest city is Fargo.

Fun Fact North Dakota leads the United States in honey production, with more than 33 million pounds (14 million kg) produced annually. In addition to honey, bees produce wax and help pollinate crops.

↑ Fossils of prehistoric life, such as this leaf, can be found in North Dakota's sedimentary rock formations.

↑ Cowboys on the fence watch the excitement of the rodeo during the Slope County Fair in Amidon.

CANADA
U.S.

MONTANA

Williston

Missouri

LITTLE

Watford City

Yellowstone

THEODORE ROOSEVELT N.P. (NORTH UNIT)

Little Missouri

MISSOURI

Theodore Roosevelt N.P. (Elkhorn Ranch Site)

Badlands

NATIONAL

THEODORE ROOSEVELT N.P. (SOUTH UNIT)

Medora

GRASSLAND

Amidon

White Butte
3,506 ft
1,069 m

Highest point in North Dakota

Cedar

Little Missouri

Hettinger

| 0 | 100 miles |
| 0 | 100 kilometers |

N

North Dakota State Flag

Wild Prairie Rose
State Flower

← American bison are native to the Great Plains, but now they are found mainly in parks such as Sullys Hill National Game Preserve.

Western Meadowlark
State Bird

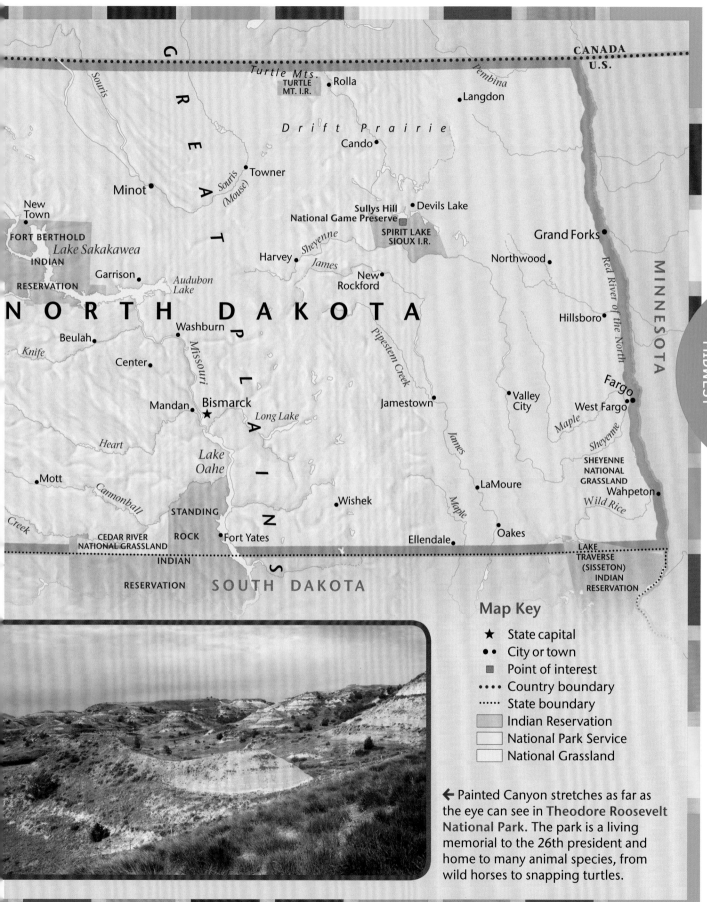

CANADA
U.S.

G R E A T

Souris

Turtle Mts.
TURTLE
MT. I.R.

• Rolla

• Langdon

D r i f t   P r a i r i e

• Cando

Minot •

• Towner

Souris
(Mouse)

New
Town

FORT BERTHOLD

Lake Sakakawea

INDIAN

RESERVATION

Garrison •

Sullys Hill
National Game Preserve

• Devils Lake

SPIRIT LAKE
SIOUX I.R.

Grand Forks •

Harvey •

Sheyenne

James

New
Rockford

•

Northwood •

Hillsboro •

A

Audubon
Lake

T

N O R T H   D A K O T A

Beulah •

Knife

Washburn •

Center •

Missouri

P

Pipestem Creek

L

Red River of the North

M I N N E S O T A

Fargo

Mandan •

★ Bismarck

Long Lake

A

Jamestown •

Valley
City •

West Fargo •

Maple

Sheyenne

Heart

Lake
Oahe

I

James

LaMoure •

SHEYENNE
NATIONAL
GRASSLAND

Mott •

Cannonball

STANDING

N

Wishek •

Maple

Wahpeton •

Wild Rice

Creek

CEDAR RIVER
NATIONAL GRASSLAND

ROCK

• Fort Yates

S

Ellendale •

Oakes •

LAKE
TRAVERSE
(SISSETON)
INDIAN
RESERVATION

INDIAN

RESERVATION   **SOUTH DAKOTA**

Map Key

★ State capital
• • City or town
■ Point of interest
•••• Country boundary
•••• State boundary
▢ Indian Reservation
▢ National Park Service
▢ National Grassland

← Painted Canyon stretches as far as
the eye can see in **Theodore Roosevelt
National Park**. The park is a living
memorial to the 26th president and
home to many animal species, from
wild horses to snapping turtles.

OHIO

Ohio

 Land & Water Wayne National Forest, Lake Erie, and the Ohio River are important land and water features of Ohio.

 Statehood Ohio became the 17th state in 1803.

People & Places Ohio's population is 11,613,423. Columbus is the state capital and the largest city.

 Fun Fact Ohio's nickname, the Buckeye State, comes from a local tree. The tree's name was derived from Native Americans, who thought its seeds looked like the eye of a male deer, or buck.

Ohio State Flag

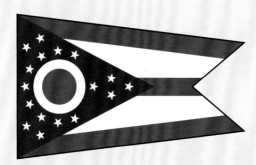

Scarlet Carnation *State Flower*

Cardinal *State Bird*

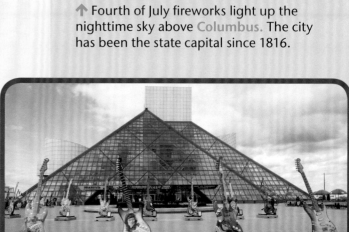

⬆ Fourth of July fireworks light up the nighttime sky above Columbus. The city has been the state capital since 1816.

⬆ Colorful guitars mark the entrance to the Rock and Roll Hall of Fame, established in downtown Cleveland in 1995.

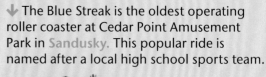 ⬇ The Blue Streak is the oldest operating roller coaster at Cedar Point Amusement Park in Sandusky. This popular ride is named after a local high school sports team.

MICHIGAN

LAKE ERIE

CANADA
U.S.

Maumee Bay

S. Bass I.

Kelleys I.

INDIANA

Toledo

Maumee

Portage

Bowling Green

Sandusky Bay

Sandusky

Lorain

N. Olmsted

Elyria

Parma

Brunswick

Medina

Mentor

Euclid

Cleveland

Shaker Heights

CUYAHOGA VALLEY N.P.

Grand

Pymatuning Reservoir

Mosquito Creek Lake

Cuyahoga Falls

Kent

Warren

Niles

PENNSYLVANIA

Auglaize

Blanchard

Findlay

Sandusky

Lima

Mansfield

Marion

Scioto

Highest point in Ohio

Campbell Hill
1,550 ft
472 m

Marysville

Urbana

O   H   I   O

Delaware

Wooster

Akron

Barberton

Massillon

Alliance

North Canton

Canton

Austintown

Youngstown

Mahoning

East Liverpool

Ohio

New Philadelphia

Tuscarawas

Coshocton

Mohican

Steubenville

Martins Ferry

St. Marys

Grand Lake (St. Marys)

Indian Lake

Upper Arlington

Westerville

Newark

Reynoldsburg

Columbus

Wills Creek

Cambridge

Zanesville

Licking

Huber Heights

Springfield

Trotwood

Dayton

Kettering

Fairborn

Xenia

Washington Court House

Middletown

Hamilton

Wilmington

Fairfield

Big Darby Cr.

Deer Cr.

Buckeye Lake

Lancaster

Muskingum

WAYNE   NATIONAL

Marietta

FOREST

Athens

Hocking

Belpre

WEST

VIRGINIA

Miami

Little Miami

Cincinnati

Ohio

East Fork Lake

E. Fk. Little Miami

Paint Creek

Hillsboro

Georgetown

Scioto

Chillicothe

Raccoon Cr.

Ohio

Gallipolis

WAYNE NATIONAL FOREST

South Point

KENTUCKY

Map Key

★ State capital
••• City or town
•••• Country boundary
•••• State boundary
▭ National Park Service
▭ National Forest land

0   50 miles
0   50 kilometers

N

→ Horse-drawn buggies are a familiar sight in **Ohio**, home to the world's largest Amish population.

South Dakota

↑ A mountain cotton-tail nibbles on some grass in **Wind Cave National Park.**

Land & Water The Black Hills, Buffalo Gap National Grassland, and the Missouri River are important land and water features of South Dakota.

Statehood South Dakota became the 40th state in 1889.

People & Places South Dakota's population is 858,469. Pierre is the state capital. The largest city is Sioux Falls.

Fun Fact A dinosaur nicknamed Sue was unearthed on the Cheyenne River Indian Reservation in 1990. It is the world's largest, most complete, and best preserved specimen of a *Tyrannosaurus rex.*

← Widespread dinosaur fossils in South Dakota prompted this humorous sign.

South Dakota State Flag

Pasqueflower
State Flower

Ring-Necked Pheasant
State Bird

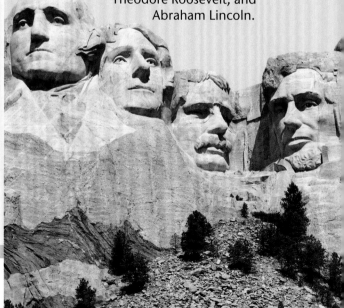

↓ Carvings on **Mount Rushmore** in the Black Hills honor four past presidents (from left to right): George Washington, Thomas Jefferson, Theodore Roosevelt, and Abraham Lincoln.

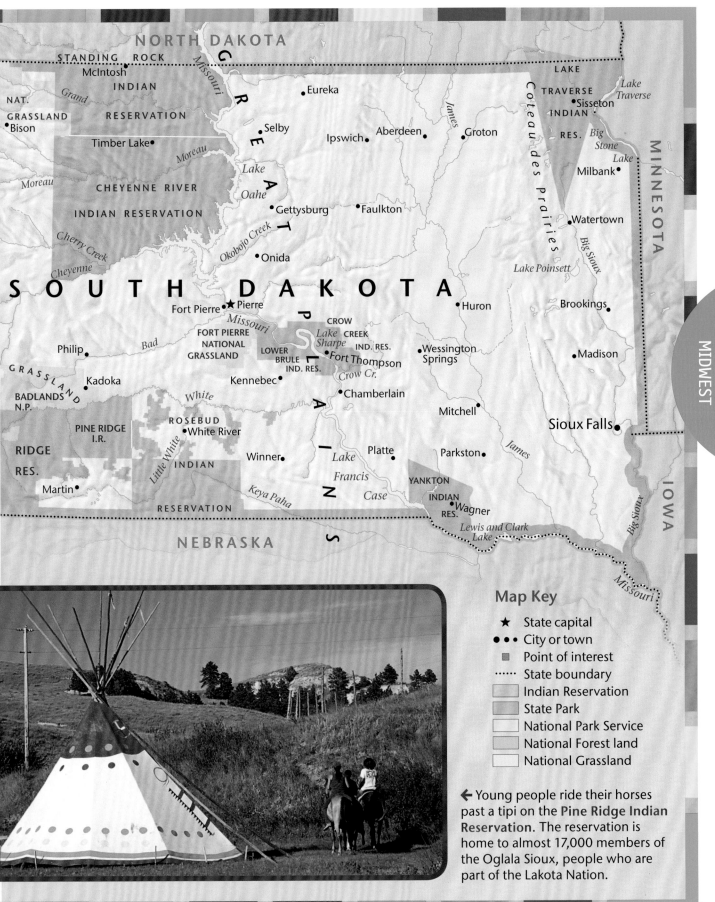

NORTH DAKOTA

STANDING ROCK

McIntosh

INDIAN

RESERVATION

NAT.
GRASSLAND

Bison

Grand

Timber Lake

Moreau

Moreau

CHEYENNE RIVER

INDIAN RESERVATION

Cherry Creek

Cheyenne

Missouri

GREAT

Eureka

Selby

Ipswich

Aberdeen

Groton

James

Lake Traverse

Sisseton

SISSETON
INDIAN
RES.

Big
Stone
Lake

Milbank

Watertown

Lake
Oahe

Gettysburg

Faulkton

Okobojo Creek

Onida

Coteau des prairies

Lake Poinsett

Big Sioux

MINNESOTA

SOUTH DAKOTA

Fort Pierre ★ Pierre

Missouri

Bad

Philip

GRASSLAND

Kadoka

BADLANDS
N.P.

PINE RIDGE
I.R.

RIDGE
RES.

Martin

FORT PIERRE
NATIONAL
GRASSLAND

LOWER
BRULE
IND. RES.

Kennebec

CROW
CREEK
IND. RES.

Lake
Sharpe

Fort Thompson

Crow Cr.

Chamberlain

White

ROSEBUD

White River

Little White

INDIAN

Winner

RESERVATION

Keya Paha

Lake
Francis
Case

Platte

Huron

Brookings

Madison

Wessington
Springs

Mitchell

Parkston

James

Sioux Falls

YANKTON
INDIAN
RES.

Wagner

Lewis and Clark
Lake

Big Sioux

IOWA

Missouri

NEBRASKA

Map Key

★ State capital
●●● City or town
■ Point of interest
•••• State boundary
■ Indian Reservation
■ State Park
□ National Park Service
■ National Forest land
□ National Grassland

← Young people ride their horses past a tipi on the **Pine Ridge Indian Reservation**. The reservation is home to almost 17,000 members of the Oglala Sioux, people who are part of the Lakota Nation.

Wisconsin

 Land & Water The Door Peninsula and Lakes Superior and Michigan are important land and water features of Wisconsin.

 Statehood
Wisconsin became the 30th state in 1848.

 People & Places
Wisconsin's population is 5,771,337. Madison is the state capital. The largest city is Milwaukee.

 Fun Fact Laura Ingalls Wilder was born in Pepin in 1867. Her famous Little House books are based on her childhood in the forests and prairies of the Midwest.

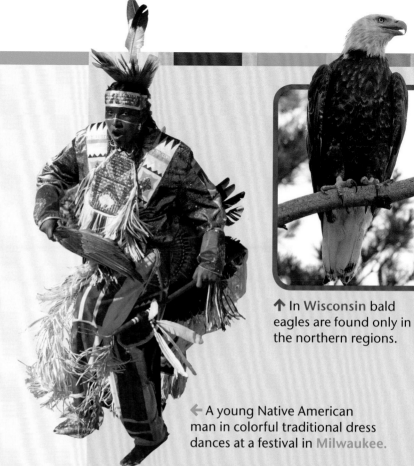

↑ In **Wisconsin** bald eagles are found only in the northern regions.

← A young Native American man in colorful traditional dress dances at a festival in **Milwaukee**.

↑ In a winter version of sailing, ice boats compete in a race on the frozen surface of **Lake Winnebago** near Oshkosh.

WISCONSIN

1848

Wisconsin State Flag

Robin
State Bird

Wood Violet
State Flower

LAKE SUPERIOR

MINNESOTA

APOSTLE ISLANDS NATIONAL LAKESHORE

Apostle Islands

RED CLIFF I.R.

Madeline Island

● Superior

Ashland ●

Bois Brule

BAD RIVER INDIAN RES.

→ Wisconsin produces more than 600 types of cheese. The town of **Monroe** celebrates Cheese Days each year.

MICHIGAN

St. Croix

Hayward ●

Lake Namekagon

ST. CROIX

NATIONAL

SCENIC

RIVERWAY

Turtle-Flambeau Flowage

LAC DU FLAMBEAU INDIAN RES.

Wisconsin

Eagle River ●

Brule

Menominee

Peshtigo

Washington Island

Lake Chippewa

LAC COURTE OREILLES I.R.

Ladysmith ●

Chippewa

Rhinelander ●

● St. Croix Falls

Red Cedar

Flambeau

Jump

Highest point in Wisconsin →

+ Timms Hill 1,951 ft 595 m

● Tomahawk

● Antigo

Marinette ●

Green Bay

● Hudson

Chippewa Falls

Yellow

● Medford

● Wausau

MENOMINEE INDIAN RES.

Oconto ●

Oconto

Sturgeon Bay ●

Door Peninsula

Menomonie ●

● Eau Claire

Big Eau Pleine Reservoir

STOCKBRIDGE-MUNSEE I.R.

Lake Du Bay

Shawano ●

Lake Pepin

W I S C O N S I N

ONEIDA INDIAN RES.

● Green Bay

Pepin ●

Chippewa

Wisconsin Rapids ●

Wisconsin

Appleton ●

Fox

● Manitowoc

Black River Falls ●

Black

Petenwell Lake

Wolf

● Neenah

Lake Poygan

Lake Winnebago

LAKE

Sparta ●

Castle Rock Lake

Oshkosh ●

● Sheboygan

● Tomah

● Viroqua

Fond du Lac ●

Milwaukee

MICHIGAN

La Crosse ●

Mississippi

Waupun ●

West Bend ●

Port Washington ●

Baraboo ●

● Portage

Fox

Beaver Dam ●

Rock

IOWA

Kickapoo

Lake Wisconsin

Menomonee Falls ●

Wauwatosa ●

Map Key

★ State capital
●●● City or town
····· State boundary
▢ Indian Reservation
▢ National Park Service
▢ National Forest land

Wisconsin

Sun Prairie ●

Lake Mendota

★ Madison

Brookfield ●

Waukesha ●

Milwaukee ●

West Allis ●

● Prairie du Chien

Stoughton ●

Platteville ●

Racine ●

Monroe ●

Janesville ●

● Kenosha

Rock

Fox

Beloit ●

Mississippi

ILLINOIS

← Wisconsin's large number of dairy farms has earned it the nickname America's Dairyland. The state dairy council is located in Brookfield.

0   50 miles

0   50 kilometers

N

The Southwest

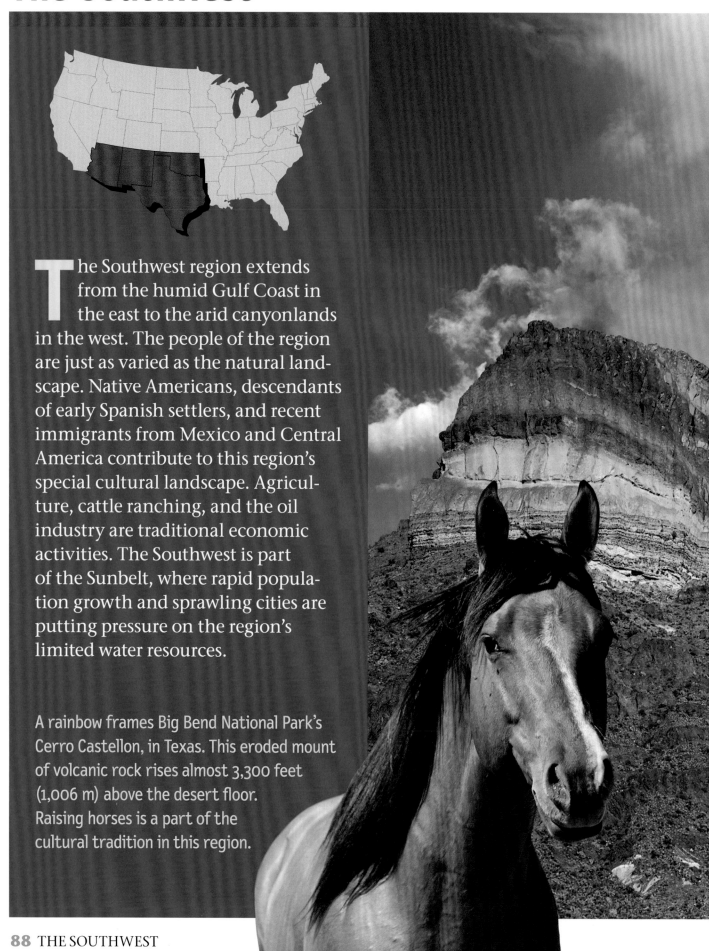

The Southwest region extends from the humid Gulf Coast in the east to the arid canyonlands in the west. The people of the region are just as varied as the natural landscape. Native Americans, descendants of early Spanish settlers, and recent immigrants from Mexico and Central America contribute to this region's special cultural landscape. Agriculture, cattle ranching, and the oil industry are traditional economic activities. The Southwest is part of the Sunbelt, where rapid population growth and sprawling cities are putting pressure on the region's limited water resources.

A rainbow frames Big Bend National Park's Cerro Castellon, in Texas. This eroded mount of volcanic rock rises almost 3,300 feet (1,006 m) above the desert floor. Raising horses is a part of the cultural tradition in this region.

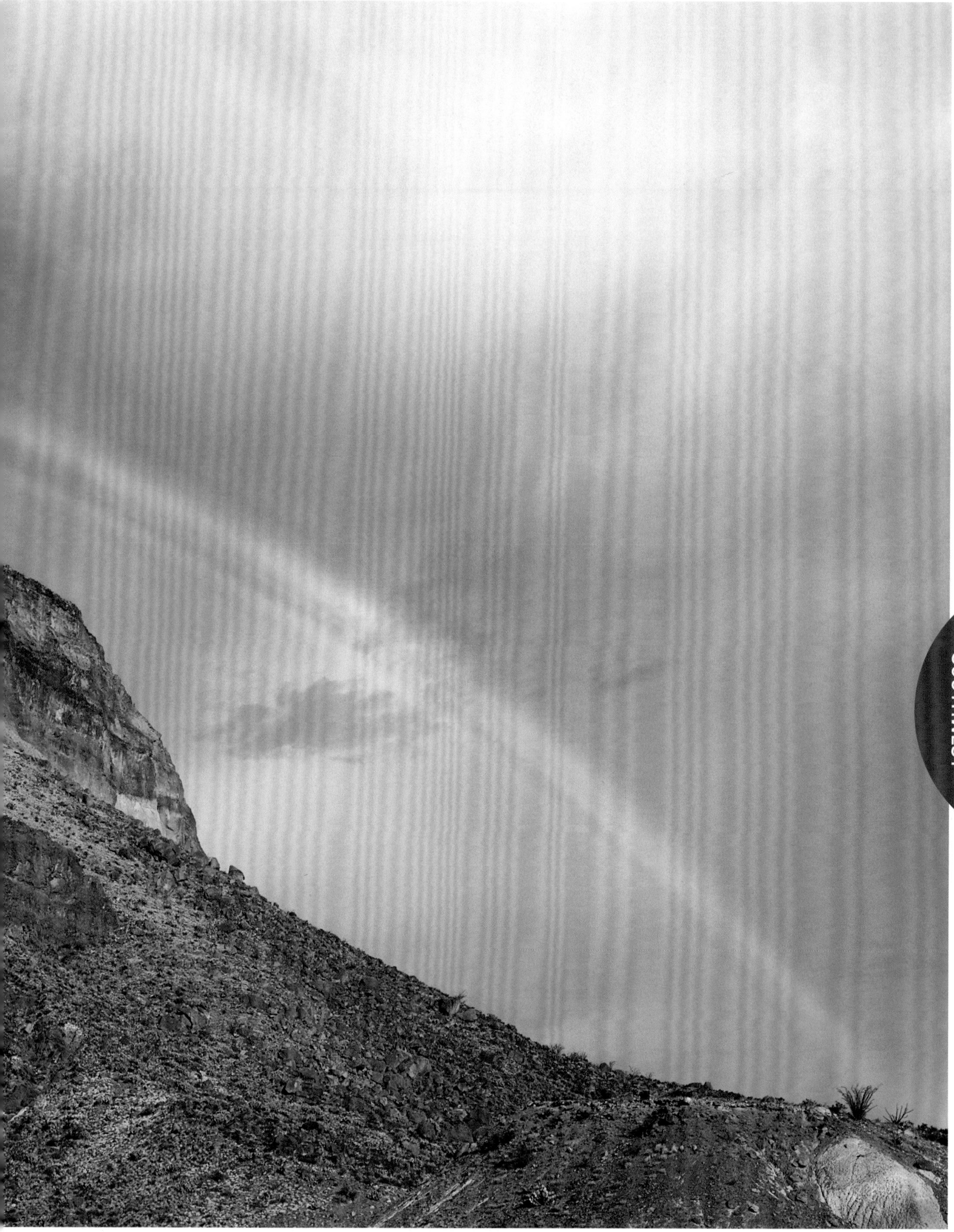

THE SOUTHWEST

Arizona

Land & Water
The Colorado Plateau, the Grand Canyon, and the Colorado River are important land and water features of Arizona.

Statehood
Arizona became the 48th state in 1912.

People & Places
Arizona's population is 6,828,065. Phoenix is the state capital and the largest city.

Fun Fact
Of the 21 Indian reservations in Arizona, the largest belongs to the Navajo Nation. Native peoples and the federal government own 70 percent of the state's land area.

↑ Daring boaters get soaked as they run the rapids on the fast-flowing waters of the **Colorado River** in Grand Canyon National Park.

↓ Saguaro cactus, found in the Sonoran Desert, can grow more than 30 feet (9 m) tall.

Arizona State Flag

Cactus Wren
State Bird

Saguaro
State Flower

N

NEVADA

UTAH

COLORADO

0 — 50 miles
0 — 50 kilometers

GLEN CANYON N.R.A.

Colorado

NAVAJO

Lake Powell

Only spot in the U.S. where the borders of four states come together

FOUR CORNERS

KAIBAB I.R.

•Page

C O L O R A D O

N A T I O N

CANYON DE CHELLY NAT. MON.

GRAND CANYON-PARASHANT NAT. MON.

Lake Mead

LAKE MEAD N.R.A.

GRAND CANYON

Grand Canyon

NATIONAL PARK

HAVASUPAI I.R.

•Grand Canyon

HOPI I.R.

HOPI INDIAN RESERVATION

I N D I A N

Fort Defiance•

LAKE MEAD

NATIONAL

RECREATION

AREA

HUALAPAI I.R.

Little Colorado

P L A T E A U

R E S E R V A T I O N

•Kingman

FT. MOJAVE I.R.

Highest point in Arizona

Humphreys Peak +
12,633 ft
3,851 m

WUPATKI N.M.

•Flagstaff

PETRIFIED FOREST N.P.

NEW MEXICO

Holbrook•

ZUNI I.R.

Little Colorado

CALIFORNIA

Colorado

Prescott•

A R I Z O N A

WHITE MOUNTAIN

APACHE INDIAN

RESERVATION

COLORADO RIVER INDIAN RESERVATION

•Quartzsite

Sun City •
Glendale •
Phoenix •
Tempe•

SALT RIVER I.R.

FT. McDOWELL I.R.

• Scottsdale
• Mesa
• Chandler

Globe•

SAN CARLOS

APACHE INDIAN

RESERVATION

S O N O R A N

GILA RIVER INDIAN RES.

Gila

Gila

MARICOPA (AK-CHIN) I.R.

GILA BEND I.R.

Colorado

Gila

•Casa Grande

•Safford

Gila

•Yuma

D E S E R T

TOHONO

O'ODHAM

Ajo•

INDIAN

ORGAN PIPE CACTUS NAT. MON.

RESERVATION

SAGUARO NAT. PARK

Tucson

TOHONO O'ODHAM (SAN XAVIER) I.R.

CHIRICAHUA NAT. MON.

U.S.
MEXICO

•Tombstone

U.S.
MEXICO

Nogales•

← Native American dancers perform in the Parada del Sol in Scottsdale. This monthlong celebration ends with rodeos and a grand parade.

Gulf of California

Map Key

★ State capital
••• City or town
■ Point of interest

•••• Country boundary
······ State boundary
Dry lake

Indian Reservation
National Park Service
National Forest land

THE SOUTHWEST

New Mexico

 Land & Water The Sangre de Cristo Mountains, Carlsbad Caverns, and the Rio Grande are important land and water features of New Mexico.

 Statehood New Mexico became the 47th state in 1912.

 People & Places New Mexico's population is 2,085,109. Santa Fe is the state capital. The largest city is Albuquerque.

 Fun Fact Roswell is a popular destination for people interested in UFOs. A local rancher discovered what he believed to be wreckage of a UFO in 1947.

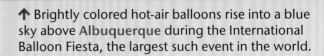

New Mexico State Flag

Yucca
State Flower

Roadrunner
State Bird

↑ Brightly colored hot-air balloons rise into a blue sky above **Albuquerque** during the International Balloon Fiesta, the largest such event in the world.

← The caves of **Carlsbad Caverns** were created as natural sulfuric acid dissolved the limestone rocks.

↓ Chili peppers, seen here in a store in **Santa Fe,** give Southwestern food a distinctive taste. New Mexico is second only to California in the production of chilies.

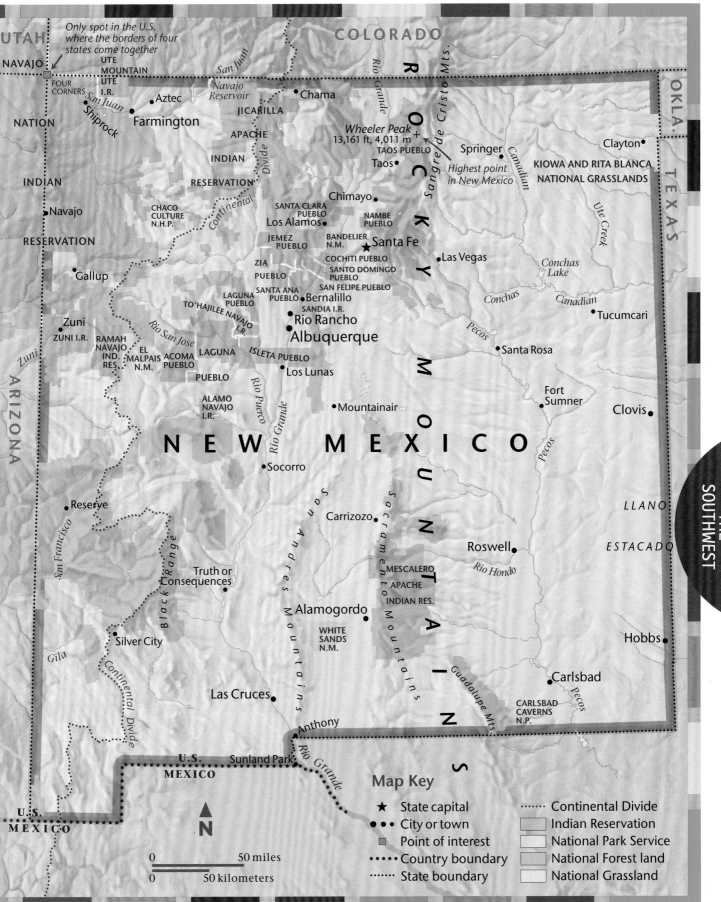

UTAH

COLORADO

OKLA.

NAVAJO

Only spot in the U.S. where the borders of four states come together

FOUR CORNERS

UTE MOUNTAIN UTE I.R.

San Juan

Navajo Reservoir

•Chama

Rio Grande

Sangre de Cristo Mts.

TEXAS

NATION

Shiprock

•Aztec

Farmington

JICARILLA

APACHE

INDIAN

RESERVATION

Wheeler Peak 13,161 ft, 4,011 m

TAOS PUEBLO

•Taos

•Springer

Canadian

Clayton•

KIOWA AND RITA BLANCA NATIONAL GRASSLANDS

INDIAN

•Navajo

CHACO CULTURE N.H.P.

Divide

Continental

Chimayo

SANTA CLARA PUEBLO

Los Alamos•

NAMBE PUEBLO

Highest point in New Mexico

Ute Creek

RESERVATION

•Gallup

JEMEZ PUEBLO

BANDELIER N.M.

★ Santa Fe

•Las Vegas

Conchas Lake

ZIA PUEBLO

COCHITI PUEBLO

SANTO DOMINGO PUEBLO

SAN FELIPE PUEBLO

Conchas

Canadian

•Tucumcari

Zuni

ZUNI I.R.

RAMAH NAVAJO IND. RES.

EL MALPAIS N.M.

TO'HAJIILEE NAVAJO I.R.

LAGUNA PUEBLO

SANTA ANA PUEBLO

•Bernalillo

SANDIA I.R.

Rio Rancho

Albuquerque

Rio San Jose

ACOMA PUEBLO

LAGUNA PUEBLO

ISLETA PUEBLO

•Los Lunas

Pecos

•Santa Rosa

Zuni

ARIZONA

ALAMO NAVAJO I.R.

Rio Puerco

Rio Grande

•Mountainair

Fort Sumner

Clovis•

NEW MEXICO

•Socorro

MOUNTAINS

Reserve•

San Francisco

Black Range

•Carrizozo

San Andres Mountains

Sacramento Mountains

LLANO

ESTACADO

Roswell•

Truth or Consequences•

MESCALERO APACHE INDIAN RES.

Rio Hondo

Pecos

Silver City•

Gila

Continental Divide

•Alamogordo

WHITE SANDS N.M.

Hobbs•

Guadalupe Mts.

•Carlsbad

Las Cruces•

Anthony•

Rio Grande

CARLSBAD CAVERNS N.P.

Pecos

U.S. MEXICO

Sunland Park•

U.S. MEXICO

N

0   50 miles

0   50 kilometers

Map Key

★ State capital

••• City or town

▪ Point of interest

•••• Country boundary

••••• State boundary

••••• Continental Divide

Indian Reservation

National Park Service

National Forest land

National Grassland

Oklahoma

COLORADO
Cimarron
Black Mesa
4,973 ft
1,516 m • Boise City H I G H Beaver
← Highest point Beaver •
in Oklahoma Optima Lake
NEW MEXICO
KIOWA AND
RITA BLANCA
NAT. GRASSLAND P L A I N S

Land & Water Black Mesa, the Ouachita Mountains, and the Arkansas River are important land and water features of Oklahoma.

Statehood Oklahoma became the 46th state in 1907.

People & Places Oklahoma's population is 3,911,338. Oklahoma City is the state capital and the largest city.

Fun Fact Before it became a state, Oklahoma was known as Indian Territory. Today 39 Indian nations, including the Cherokee, Creek, Osage, and Choctaw, have their headquarters in the state.

↑ A tornado is a destructive rotating column of air that forms from a thunderstorm. In 1974 five tornadoes struck **Oklahoma City** in one day.

OKLAHOMA

Oklahoma State Flag

Mistletoe
State Flower

Scissor-Tailed Flycatcher
State Bird

↑ The Golden Driller, with his hand on an oil rig, stands 76 feet (23 m) tall near the State Fairgrounds in **Tulsa**.

KANSAS

MISSOURI

•Buffalo

Great
Salt Plains
Lake

Salt Fork

Arkansas

OSAGE

Ponca
City

Kaw
Lake

NATION

Pawhuska

Miami

Lake O' The
Cherokees

Bartlesville

Vinita

Verdigris

Rock Creek

INDIAN

Woodward•

North Canadian

Fairview•

Enid

Sooner
Lake

Oologah
Lake

Cimarron

Canadian

Stillwater

Keystone
Lake

RES.

Skiatook
Lake

Owasso•

Tulsa
Broken
Arrow

Pryor•

Lake
Hudson

Ft. Gibson
Lake

Illinois

Bixby•

Tahlequah

OZARK

PLATEAU

ARKANSAS

OKLAHOMA

BLACK KETTLE
NATIONAL
GRASSLAND

Clinton•

El Reno•

Edmond•

★Oklahoma City

Deep Fork

Muskogee•
Okmulgee•

Tenkiller
Lake

Sallisaw

Washita

Moore•

Shawnee•

N. Canadian

Arkansas

Sayre•

North Fork

Norman•

Little

Seminole•

Eufaula
Lake

Robert
S. Kerr
Lake

Poteau•

Elm Fork

Hobart•

Chickasha•

Mangum•

Anadarko•

Purcell•

Hollis•

Salt Fork

Canadian

McAlester•

Heavener•

Wichita Mts.

Lawton•

Pauls Valley•

Ada•

Sardis
Lake

Kiamichi

Ouachita Mountains

Prairie
Dog Town Fork

Frederick•

Walters•

Washita

Sulphur•
CHICKASAW
N.R.A.

McGee Cr.
Lake

Atoka•

Broken Bow
Lake

Red

Duncan•

Arbuckle Mts.

Ardmore•

Lake
Texoma

Durant•

Hugo•

Hugo
Lake

Idabel•

TEXAS

Red

Red

THE
SOUTHWEST

N

0   50 miles
0   50 kilometers

Map Key

★ State capital
••• City or town
····· State boundary
☐ Indian Reservation
☐ National Park Service
☐ National Forest land
☐ National Grassland

← Young girls wearing
traditional dress reflect the
strong Native American
heritage in **Oklahoma**.

→ The collared lizard
is Oklahoma's state
reptile. The lizard is
common in the Wichita
Mountains and
throughout the state.

TEXAS

Texas

Land & Water The Edwards Plateau, Padre Island National Seashore, and the Rio Grande are important land and water features of Texas.

Statehood Texas became the 28th state in 1845.

People & Places The population of Texas is 27,469,114. Austin is the state capital. The largest city is Houston.

Fun Fact Over the course of its history, six different national flags have flown over Texas— Spanish, French, Mexican, Texan, Confederate, and American.

Texas State Flag

Mockingbird
State Bird

Bluebonnet
State Flower

↑ The brightly lit Congress Avenue Bridge crosses Town Lake into downtown Austin, where tall buildings rise against the night sky.

NEW MEXICO

ROCKY
MEXICO
U.S.
Rio Grande
Davis Mts.
M

GUADALUPE MTS. N.P.

El Paso

+Guadalupe Peak
Highest point in Texas
8,749 ft
2,667 m

Presidio

← Texas leads the United States in oil and natural gas production. A well near Houston pumps oil, called "black gold" because it's worth so much money.

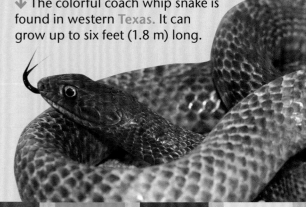

↓ The colorful coach whip snake is found in western Texas. It can grow up to six feet (1.8 m) long.

KIOWA AND
RITA BLANCA
NAT. GRASSLAND

HIGH PLAINS

Dumas •

LAKE MEREDITH N.R.A.

Pampa •

Canadian

Amarillo

• Hereford

N. Fork

Salt Fork

Childress •

→ Riders on horseback pass by the Alamo in **San Antonio** during Fiesta San Jacinto. The Alamo is an important historic landmark.

OKLAHOMA

ARKANSAS

Plainview •

Cap Rock Escarpment

Vernon •

Red

Wichita

Lake Texoma

L L A N O

Lubbock •

Wichita Falls

Sherman •

CADDO NAT. GRASSLAND

Paris •

Red

Texarkana •

E S T A C A D O

• Brownfield

Brazos

LYNDON B. JOHNSON N.G.

Denton

Plano

Irving

Garland

• Lamesa

Fort Worth

Arlington

Dallas

Longview •

Abilene

Brazos

Tyler •

Toledo Bend Reservoir

• Midland

• Odessa

Brownwood •

Colorado

Waco

Nacogdoches

Trinity

Lufkin •

• Pecos

San Angelo •

T E X A S

Temple •

Sam Rayburn Res.

Pecos

Copperas Cove •

Killeen •

Huntsville •

Bryan •

College Station

BIG THICKET NATIONAL PRESERVE

Sabine

Fort Stockton •

E d w a r d s

Georgetown •

Round Rock •

Conroe •

Beaumont

Baytown

P l a t e a u

★ **Austin**

Port Arthur •

Houston

THE SOUTHWEST

H i l l   C o u n t r y

AMISTAD N.R.A.

Amistad Reservoir

San Marcos •

New Braunfels •

San Antonio •

Guadalupe

Sugar Land

Bay City •

• Galveston

BIG BEND NATIONAL PARK

• Del Rio

U.S.

MEXICO

Victoria •

• Freeport

San Antonio

• Port Lavaca

Eagle Pass •

Nueces

• Beeville

• Rockport

Rio Grande

Map Key

★ State capital

•••• City or town

••••• Country boundary

•••••• State boundary

Swamp

National Park Service

National Forest land

National Grassland

Alice •

Corpus Christi •

G U L F   O F   M E X I C O

Laredo •

Kingsville •

PADRE ISLAND NATIONAL SEASHORE

Falcon Reservoir

Rio Grande City •

McAllen

Harlingen •

Mission •

U.S.

MEXICO

Brownsville

0   100 miles

0   100 kilometers

N

The West

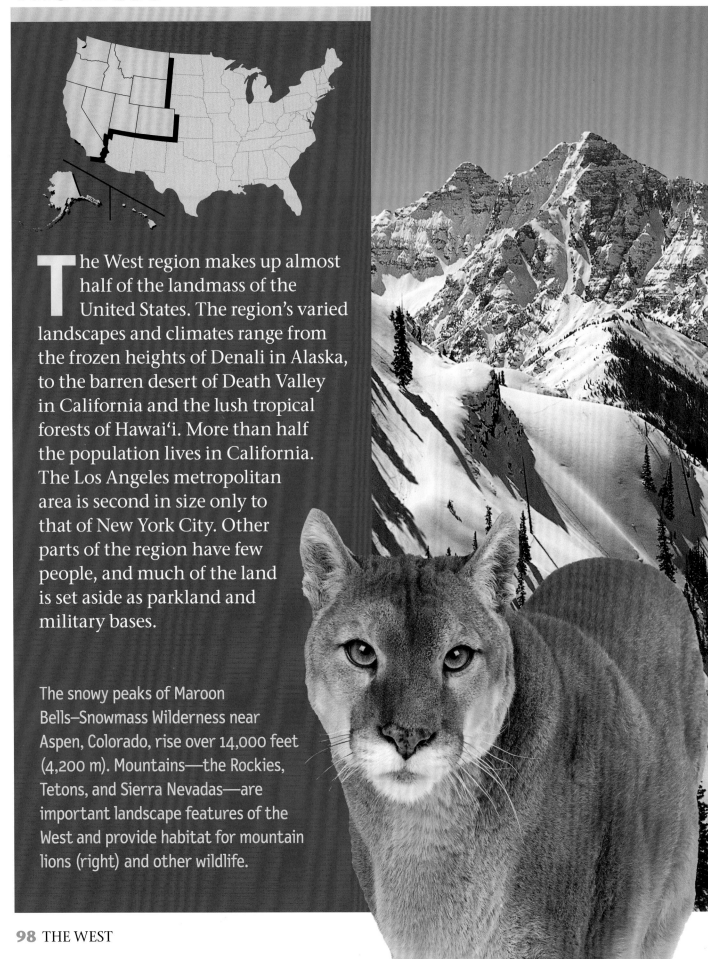

The West region makes up almost half of the landmass of the United States. The region's varied landscapes and climates range from the frozen heights of Denali in Alaska, to the barren desert of Death Valley in California and the lush tropical forests of Hawai'i. More than half the population lives in California. The Los Angeles metropolitan area is second in size only to that of New York City. Other parts of the region have few people, and much of the land is set aside as parkland and military bases.

The snowy peaks of Maroon Bells–Snowmass Wilderness near Aspen, Colorado, rise over 14,000 feet (4,200 m). Mountains—the Rockies, Tetons, and Sierra Nevadas—are important landscape features of the West and provide habitat for mountain lions (right) and other wildlife.

The West

Alaska

 Land & Water The Tongass National Forest, Brooks Range, and the Yukon River are important land and water features of Alaska.

 Statehood Alaska became the 49th state in 1959.

 People & Places Alaska's population is 738,432. Juneau is the state capital. The largest city is Anchorage.

 **Fun Fact** The most powerful earthquake ever recorded in North America struck Anchorage in 1964. Eighty times more powerful than the 1906 San Francisco earthquake, it measured 9.2 on the Richter scale.

Alaska State Flag

Forget-Me-Not *State Flower*

Willow Ptarmigan *State Bird*

↑ Dogsledding has a long and colorful history in Alaska. The most famous race is the Iditarod, which runs from Anchorage to **Nome** along an old mail and supply route.

CHUKCHI

RUSSIA

Bering

St. Lawrence I.

St. Matthew I.

Nunivak I.

BERING SEA

St. Paul • Pribilof Islands

ALEUTIAN ISLANDS
Unimak I.
Unalaska I.
Umnak I. •Unalaska
Islands of Four Mountains
Yunaska I.

Continuation of the Aleutian Islands on map to the right

PACIFIC OCEAN

← Native peoples in Alaska carved totem poles to tell their histories. Carvers still make totem poles at Saxman Native Village in **Ketchikan**.

ARCTIC OCEAN

Barrow • Point Barrow ← Northernmost point in the U.S.

BEAUFORT SEA

SEA

Prudhoe Bay

North Slope

Meade

BROOKS RANGE

Colville

Point Hope

NOATAK NAT. PRESERVE

RUSSIA
U.S.

CAPE KRUSENSTERN NAT. MON.

Strait

Little Diomede I.

KOBUK VALLEY N.P.

GATES OF THE ARCTIC NAT. PARK & PRESERVE

Porcupine

ARCTIC CIRCLE

Kotzebue

CANADA
U.S.

Cape Prince of Wales

BERING LAND BRIDGE NAT. PRES.

Fort Yukon

Seward Peninsula

Nome

Galena

Yukon

Fairbanks

North Pole

YUKON-CHARLEY RIVERS NAT. PRES.

Norton Sound

ALASKA

Yukon Delta

Unalakleet

IDITAROD

Kuskokwim Mountains

RANGE

Tanana

Highest point in North America

Yukon

DENALI NATIONAL PARK & PRES.

Mountain Village

Yukon

IDITAROD HISTORIC TRAIL

Denali (Mt.McKinley) 20,310 ft 6,190 m

WRANGELL-ST. ELIAS NAT.

Hooper Bay

Aniak

Kuskokwim River

ALASKA RANGE

Palmer

Chugach Mts.

PARK & PRES.

St. Elias Mountains

Skagway

COAST MOUNTAINS

Nelson I.

Anchorage

Kenai

Valdez

Mt. St. Elias 18,008 ft 5,489 m

LAKE CLARK N.P. & PRES.

Kenai Peninsula

Prince William Sound

TONGASS N.F.

Iliamna Lake

Cook Inlet

Seward

GLACIER BAY N.P. & PRESERVE

Juneau

ALASKA PENINSULA

KENAI FJORDS NAT. PARK

GULF OF ALASKA

TONGASS

KATMAI N.P. & PRESERVE

Afognak Island

Chichagof I.

Petersburg

Aleutian Range

Bristol Bay

Kodiak

ALEXANDER

Sitka

NAT. FOR.

Kodiak Island

Baranof I.

Wrangell

ANIAKCHAK NAT. MON. & PRESERVE

ARCHIPELAGO

Ketchikan

Trinity Islands

Prince of Wales I.

ANNETTE ISLAND I.R.

Peaked I. Attu I. ALEUTIAN ISLANDS Yunaska I.

U.S.
CANADA

NEAR IS.

Dixon Entrance

Agattu I.

Kiska

Seguam I.

Sanak I.

Although in the Eastern Hemisphere, Peaked Island is considered to be the westernmost point in the United States.

I. RAT ISLANDS

Semisopochnoi Island

Tanaga I.

Atka I.

Amlia I.

Continuation of the Aleutian Islands at same scale as main map

Adak I.

Amchitka I.

ANDREANOF ISLANDS

N

Map Key

★ State capital
••• City or town
- - - National trail
•••• Country boundary
▭ Indian Reservation
▭ National Park Service
▭ National Forest land

| 0 | 200 miles |
| 0 | 200 kilometers |

↓ Many types of crabs are found in Alaska. Golden king crabs live in waters around the Aleutian Islands in southwest Alaska.

CALIFORNIA

California

 Land & Water The Sierra Nevada, Death Valley, and San Francisco Bay are important land and water features of California.

 Statehood California became the 31st state in 1850.

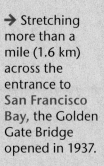 **People & Places** California's population is 39,144,818. Sacramento is the state capital. The largest city is Los Angeles.

 Fun Fact Death Valley is the hottest place in the United States. In July 1913 what is now Furnace Creek Ranch registered a temperature of 134°F (57°C).

→ Stretching more than a mile (1.6 km) across the entrance to **San Francisco Bay**, the Golden Gate Bridge opened in 1937.

↑ An elephant seal on one of California's **Channel Islands** roars at a photographer who has invaded the seal's territory on the beach.

↓ In **Leggett**, automobiles can drive through the base of this redwood tree, nicknamed the Chandelier Tree because of its huge branches.

California State Flag

CALIFORNIA REPUBLIC

Golden Poppy
State Flower

California Quail
State Bird

Chandelier Tree
Height 315 ft. Diameter 21 ft.
Maximum Age 2400 yrs.
DRIVE-THRU TREE PARK Leggett CA

OREGON

IDAHO

Crescent City

REDWOOD NATIONAL PARK

HOOPA VALLEY I.R.

LAVA BEDS NAT. MON.

WHISKEYTOWN N.R.A.

Eureka

LASSEN VOLCANIC N.P.

Susanville

Leggett

Redding

ROUND VALLEY I.R.

Chico

Ukiah

Lake Tahoe

↑ California produces almost all the artichokes grown in the United States. Castroville claims the title of Artichoke Center of the World.

Santa Rosa

Sacramento ★

Mono Lake

Vallejo

Stockton

YOSEMITE NATIONAL PARK

NEVADA

San Francisco

Oakland

Modesto

San Francisco Bay

San Jose

N

Santa Cruz

Monterey Bay

Castroville

San Joaquin

KINGS CANYON NAT. PARK

DEATH

Highest point in the 48 contiguous states

Monterey

Salinas

Fresno

Lowest point in North America; highest recorded temperature in the U.S., 134°F (57°C)

PINNACLES N.P.

SEQUOIA N.P.

VALLEY

+ Mt. Whitney 14,494 ft, 4,418 m

-282 ft

-86 m

PACIFIC

Visalia

TULE RIVER I.R.

NATIONAL

OCEAN

Paso Robles

Bakersfield

PARK · Ridgecrest

DESERT

MOJAVE NAT. PRESERVE

Barstow

FORT MOJAVE I.R.

Lake Havasu

Map Key

★ State capital

Lancaster

CHEMEHUEVI I.R.

•••• City or town

Pasadena

San Bernardino

COLORADO RIVER I.R.

---- National trail

Santa Barbara

•••• Country boundary

SANTA MONICA MTS. N.R.A.

Palm Springs

JOSHUA TREE NAT. PARK

SONORAN

•••• State boundary

CHANNEL ISLANDS NATIONAL PARK

Oxnard

Riverside

AGUA CALIENTE I.R.

Blythe

Dry lake

Santa Monica

Los Angeles

Anaheim

Salton Sea

Sand

Long Beach

Santa Ana

PALA I.R.

LOS COYOTES I.R.

DESERT

Lava

Oceanside

Imperial Valley

FORT YUMA I.R.

Area below sea level

Escondido

CAPITAN GRANDE I.R.

El Centro

Indian Reservation

National Park Service

0   100 miles

San Diego

National Forest land

0   100 kilometers

Colorado

U.S. MEXICO

Colorado

Land & Water The Rocky Mountains, Roosevelt National Forest, and the Colorado River are important land and water features of Colorado.

Statehood Colorado became the 38th state in 1876.

People & Places Colorado's population is 5,456,574. Denver is the state capital and the largest city.

Fun Fact The 700-foot (210-m)-high sand dunes in Great Sand Dunes National Park and Preserve occupy an area that was covered by an ancient sea more than a million years ago.

↑ Bighorn sheep, known for their large curled horns, live in **Rocky Mountain National Park** and other mountainous areas of the West.

↓ Early native people built more than 600 stone structures into cliff walls that are now part of **Mesa Verde National Park.**

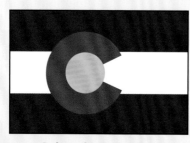

Colorado State Flag

Columbine
State Flower

Lark Bunting
State Bird

Map labels: COLORADO · Green · DINOSAUR NATIONAL MONUMENT · Danforth · White · Rangely · Cathedral Bluffs · Roan Plateau · Grand Valley · Grand Junction · UTAH · Colorado · COLORADO NAT. MON. · Grand · Dolores · Uncompahgre · San Miguel · Cortez · MESA VERDE N.P. · UTE MOUNTAIN I.R. · Mancos · FOUR CORNERS · San Juan · ARIZONA · Only spot in the U.S. where the borders of four states come together

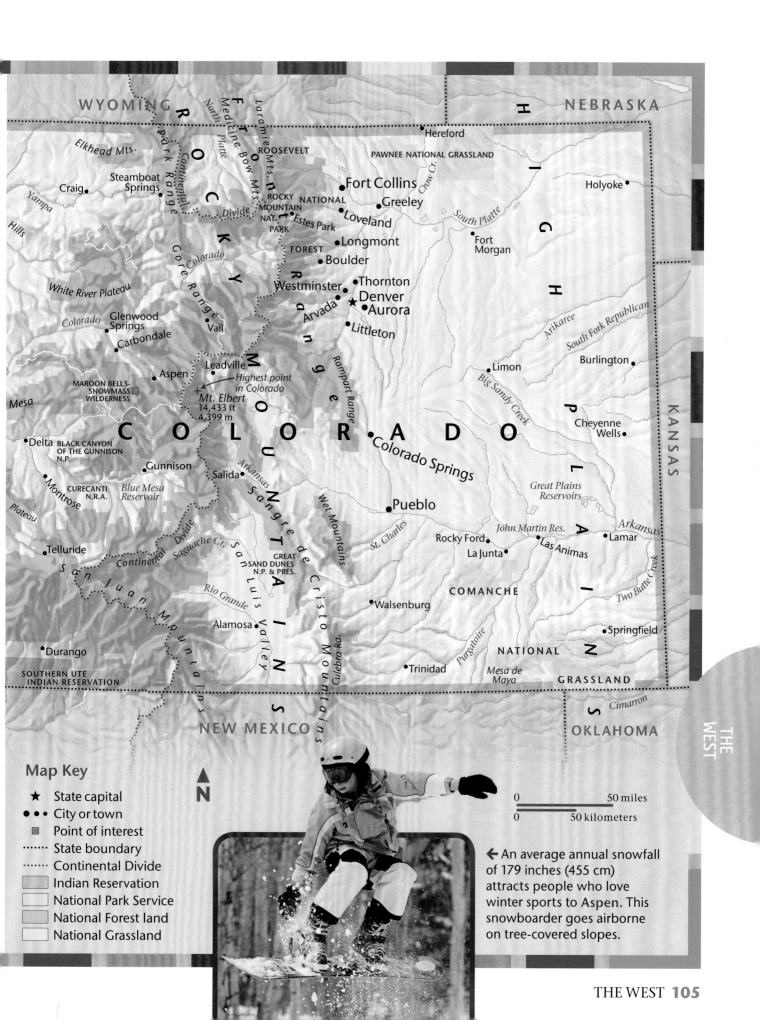

WYOMING
NEBRASKA

Elkhead Mts.

Craig

Steamboat Springs

Hereford

PAWNEE NATIONAL GRASSLAND

Fort Collins

Greeley

Holyoke

ROCKY MOUNTAIN NATIONAL

Loveland

Estes Park

Longmont

FOREST

Boulder

Fort Morgan

White River Plateau

Westminster

Thornton

Denver

Arvada

Aurora

Littleton

Glenwood Springs

Vail

Carbondale

Limon

Burlington

Aspen

Leadville

Highest point in Colorado

Cheyenne Wells

MAROON BELLS-SNOWMASS WILDERNESS

Mt. Elbert 14,433 ft 4,399 m

Mesa

COLORADO

Colorado Springs

Delta

BLACK CANYON OF THE GUNNISON N.P.

Gunnison

Salida

Great Plains Reservoirs

Montrose

CURECANTI N.R.A.

Blue Mesa Reservoir

John Martin Res.

Arkansas

Plateau

Pueblo

Rocky Ford

La Junta

Las Animas

Lamar

Telluride

Continental Divide

GREAT SAND DUNES N.P. & PRES.

St. Charles

COMANCHE

Two Butte Creek

Alamosa

Walsenburg

Springfield

Durango

SOUTHERN UTE INDIAN RESERVATION

NATIONAL

GRASSLAND

Trinidad

Mesa de Maya

NEW MEXICO

Cimarron

OKLAHOMA

Map Key

★ State capital

••• City or town

■ Point of interest

...... State boundary

...... Continental Divide

Indian Reservation

National Park Service

National Forest land

National Grassland

N

0   50 miles

0   50 kilometers

← An average annual snowfall of 179 inches (455 cm) attracts people who love winter sports to **Aspen**. This snowboarder goes airborne on tree-covered slopes.

The West

Hawai'i

Land & Water Kilauea crater, Diamond Head, and Pearl Harbor are important land and water features of Hawai'i.

Statehood Hawai'i became the 50th state in 1959.

People & Places Hawai'i's population is 1,431,603. Honolulu is the state capital and the largest city.

Fun Fact Hawai'i is the fastest growing state in the United States—not in people, but in land. Active volcanoes are constantly creating new land as lava flows into the sea.

KAUA'I

Wai'ale'ale
5,148 ft
1,569 m

WAIMEA CANYON

Kaulakahi Channel

Lehua

Pu'uwai

Kekaha

Kalaheo

Kapa'a

Lihu'e

NI'IHAU

Kaua'i

← Pu'u 'Ō'ō vent on **Kilauea crater** has added more than 568 acres (230 ha) of new land to Hawai'i.

P A C I F I C

↓ Hawai'i is the leading pineapple producer in the United States. Pineapples are grown on Lāna'i, Maui, and O'ahu.

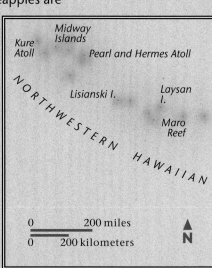

Kure Atoll

Midway Islands

Pearl and Hermes Atoll

Lisianski I.

Laysan I.

Maro Reef

N O R T H W E S T E R N   H A W A I I A N

0   200 miles
0   200 kilometers

N

Hawai'i State Flag

Hibiscus
State Flower

Hawaiian Goose (Nene)
State Bird

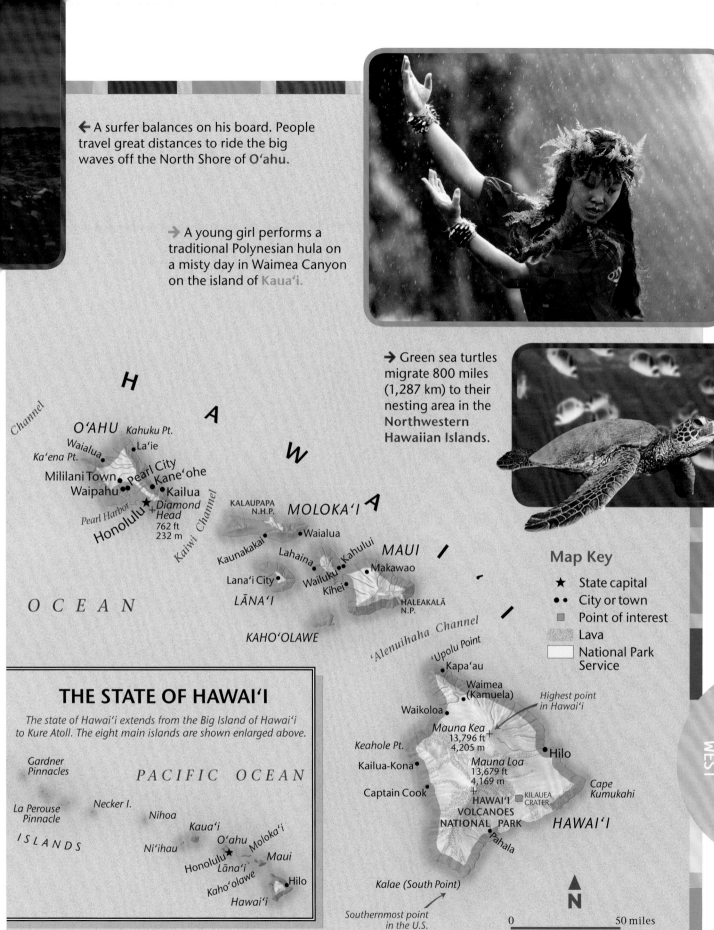

← A surfer balances on his board. People travel great distances to ride the big waves off the North Shore of **Oʻahu**.

→ A young girl performs a traditional Polynesian hula on a misty day in Waimea Canyon on the island of **Kauaʻi**.

→ Green sea turtles migrate 800 miles (1,287 km) to their nesting area in the Northwestern Hawaiian Islands.

Map Key

★ State capital
●● City or town
■ Point of interest
░ Lava
□ National Park Service

THE STATE OF HAWAIʻI

The state of Hawaiʻi extends from the Big Island of Hawaiʻi to Kure Atoll. The eight main islands are shown enlarged above.

PACIFIC OCEAN

Gardner Pinnacles

La Perouse Pinnacle

Necker I.

Nihoa

Niʻihau

Kauaʻi

Oʻahu

Honolulu ★

Lānaʻi

Kahoʻolawe

Molokaʻi

Maui

Hilo

Hawaiʻi

ISLANDS

Map labels

H A W A I I

Channel

OʻAHU
Kahuku Pt.
Waialua
Kaʻena Pt. • Laʻie
Mililani Town • Pearl City
Waipahu • • Kaneʻohe
Pearl Harbor • Kailua
Honolulu + Diamond Head
762 ft 232 m
Kaiwi Channel

KALAUPAPA N.H.P.
MOLOKAʻI
• Waialua
Kaunakakai
Lahaina • Kahului
Lanaʻi City • Wailuku • Makawao
LĀNAʻI • Kihei
MAUI
HALEAKALĀ N.P.
KAHOʻOLAWE
ʻAlenuihaha Channel

OCEAN

ʻUpolu Point
• Kapaʻau
• Waimea (Kamuela)
Highest point in Hawaiʻi
• Waikoloa
Mauna Kea + 13,796 ft 4,205 m
Keahole Pt.
Mauna Loa 13,679 ft 4,169 m
Kailua-Kona •
Captain Cook • + HAWAIʻI ■ KILAUEA CRATER
Cape Kumukahi
VOLCANOES NATIONAL PARK
• Hilo
HAWAIʻI
• Pahala
Kalae (South Point)
Southernmost point in the U.S.

0 — 50 miles
0 — 50 kilometers

N

IDAHO

Idaho

 Land & Water The Bitterroot Range, the Columbia Plateau, and the Snake River are important land and water features of Idaho.

 Statehood Idaho became the 43rd state in 1890.

 People & Places Idaho's population is 1,654,930. Boise is the state capital and the largest city.

Fun Fact In preparation for their mission to the moon, American astronauts visited Craters of the Moon National Monument and Preserve to study its volcanic geology and experience its harsh environment.

↑ A wood duck perches on a post. These colorful waterfowl can be viewed in Kootenai National Wildlife Refuge near **Bonners Ferry**.

↑ More than 40 percent of Idaho's land area is forested. Use of this land is overseen by the Forest Products Commission in **Boise**. Forest products are important to the state's economy.

Idaho State Flag

Syringa (Mock Orange)
State Flower

Mountain Bluebird
State Bird

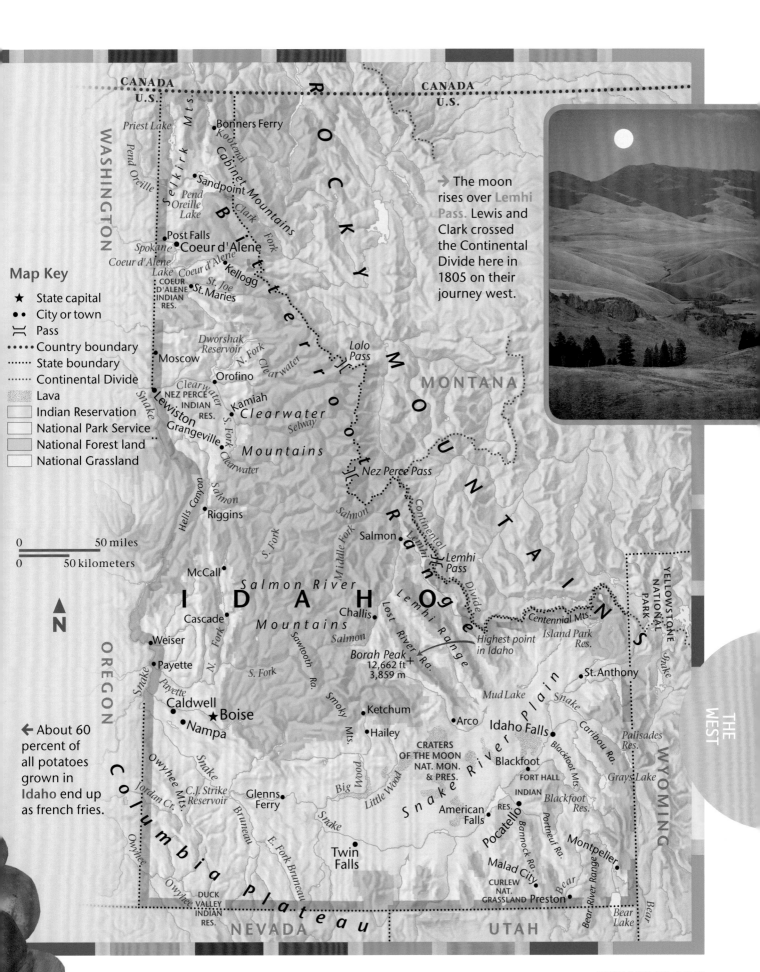

Map Key

- ★ State capital
- •• City or town
-)(Pass
- •••• Country boundary
- ····· State boundary
- ····· Continental Divide
- Lava
- Indian Reservation
- National Park Service
- National Forest land
- National Grassland

→ The moon rises over **Lemhi Pass.** Lewis and Clark crossed the Continental Divide here in 1805 on their journey west.

← About 60 percent of all potatoes grown in **Idaho** end up as french fries.

CANADA
U.S.

CANADA
U.S.

WASHINGTON

Priest Lake

Bonners Ferry

Selkirk Mts.

Kootenai

Cabinet Mountains

Pend Oreille

Pend Oreille Lake

Post Falls

Spokane

Coeur d'Alene

Coeur d'Alene Lake

COEUR D'ALENE INDIAN RES.

Coeur d'Alene

Kellogg

St. Joe

St. Maries

Clark Fork

R O C K Y

Dworshak Reservoir

Moscow

Orofino

N. Fork

Clearwater

Lolo Pass

Clearwater

NEZ PERCE INDIAN RES.

Lewiston

Kamiah

Clearwater

Selway

Grangeville

S. Fork

Clearwater

Mountains

Bitterroot

MONTANA

Nez Perce Pass

Salmon

Continental

Snake

Hells Canyon

Salmon

Riggins

S. Fork

Middle Fork

Salmon

Lemhi

Salmon

Challis

Lemhi Pass

M O U N T A I N S

Divide

Centennial Mts.

YELLOWSTONE NATIONAL PARK

McCall

I D A H O

Salmon River

Lost River Ra.

Lemhi Range

Island Park Res.

Cascade

Mountains

Salmon

Snake

Weiser

N. Fork

Borah Peak + 12,662 ft 3,859 m

Highest point in Idaho

St. Anthony

Payette

Sawtooth Ra.

Smoky Mts.

Snake River Plain

Caribou Ra.

Palisades Res.

Payette

Caldwell

★ Boise

Nampa

S. Fork

Ketchum

Hailey

Arco

Idaho Falls

Mud Lake

Snake

W Y O M I N G

CRATERS OF THE MOON NAT. MON. & PRES.

Blackfoot

Blackfoot Mts.

Grays Lake

Owyhee Mts.

Snake

Jordan Cr.

C.J. Strike Reservoir

Glenns Ferry

Big Wood

Little Wood

American Falls

FORT HALL INDIAN RES.

Blackfoot Res.

Bruneau

Snake

Pocatello

Bannock Ra.

Portneuf Ra.

Montpelier

Owyhee

Twin Falls

Bear

Bear-River Range

Malad City

CURLEW NAT. GRASSLAND

Preston

Bear

Columbia Plateau

E. Fork Bruneau

DUCK VALLEY INDIAN RES.

NEVADA

UTAH

Bear Lake

0 ——— 50 miles
0 ——— 50 kilometers

N

Montana

Land & Water The Rocky Mountains, the Great Plains, and the Yellowstone River are important land and water features of Montana.

Statehood Montana became the 41st state in 1889.

People & Places Montana's population is 1,032,949. Helena is the state capital. The largest city is Billings.

Fun Fact Montana is the only state with river systems that empty into the Gulf of Mexico to the southeast, Hudson Bay in Canada, and the Pacific Ocean to the west.

MONTANA

Montana State Flag

Bitterroot
State Flower

Western Meadowlark
State Bird

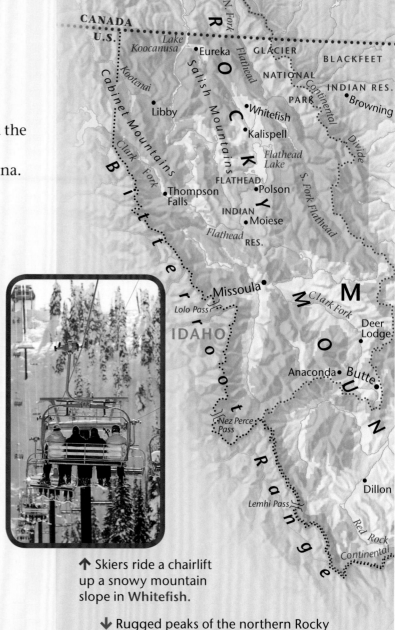

↑ Skiers ride a chairlift up a snowy mountain slope in **Whitefish**.

↓ Rugged peaks of the northern Rocky Mountains are reflected in the still surface of a mountain lake in **Glacier National Park**.

CANADA
U.S.

CANADA
U.S.

Cut Bank

Chinook

Scobey •

Plentywood •

Milk

Havre

Malta

FORT
BELKNAP
INDIAN
RESERVATION

Milk

FORT PECK
INDIAN RESERVATION

Marias

ROCKY BOYS
I.R.

Glasgow •

Wolf Point •

Missouri

Sidney •

Teton

Fort Benton •

Missouri

Fort Peck Lake

Circle •

Yellowstone

Great Falls •

Jordan •

Glendive •

Wibaux •

O   N   T   A   N   A

Lewistown •

Terry •

★ Helena

Canyon Ferry L.

Roundup •

Musselshell

Miles City •

Baker •

Townsend •

Missouri

Forsyth •

Yellowstone

Tongue

Big Timber •

Billings •

Colstrip •

Jefferson

Madison

Gallatin

• Bozeman

Columbus •

Clarks Fk.

Hardin •
Crow Agency •

Bighorn

CROW INDIAN
RESERVATION

NORTHERN
CHEYENNE
I.R.

Powder

Broadus •

*Highest point
in Montana*

Little Missouri

Virginia City •

Granite Peak
12,799 ft
3,901 m

• Red Lodge

BIGHORN CANYON
N.R.A.

Bighorn

T
A
I
N
S

Yellowstone

Absaroka Range

West

Yellowstone

Divide

YELLOWSTONE

NATIONAL

PARK

Mountains

WYOMING

NORTH DAKOTA

SOUTH DAKOTA

G   R   E   A   T   P   L   A   I   N   S

0   50 miles
0   50 kilometers

N

Map Key

★ State capital
•• City or town
⊐⊏ Pass
•••• Country boundary
•••••• State boundary
•••••• Continental Divide
▭ Indian Reservation
▭ National Park Service
▭ National Forest land

→ Many people
want the experience
of living on a ranch.
One family-oriented
ranch near **Bozeman**
has special programs
for children.

↓ American bison are protected
in the National Bison Range, a
wildlife refuge near Moiese.

Nevada

Land & Water The Great Basin, the Mojave Desert, and Lake Mead are important land and water features of Nevada.

Statehood Nevada became the 36th state in 1864.

People & Places Nevada's population is 2,890,845. Carson City is the state capital. The largest city is Las Vegas.

Fun Fact Kangaroo rats, which live in the Mojave Desert and other arid areas of the West, are small, seed-eating rodents that can survive with little or no water.

↑ The Luxor, re-creating a scene from ancient Egypt, is one of the many lavish hotels that attract millions of tourists to **Las Vegas**.

← Paiute Indians, dressed in traditional clothing, live on the Pyramid Lake Reservation near **Reno**. Their economy centers on fishing, camping, and other recreational activities.

↓ The desert environment of Nevada includes many plants that tolerate very dry conditions. The setting sun highlights mountains in the distance.

Nevada State Flag

Mountain Bluebird
State Bird

Sagebrush
State Flower

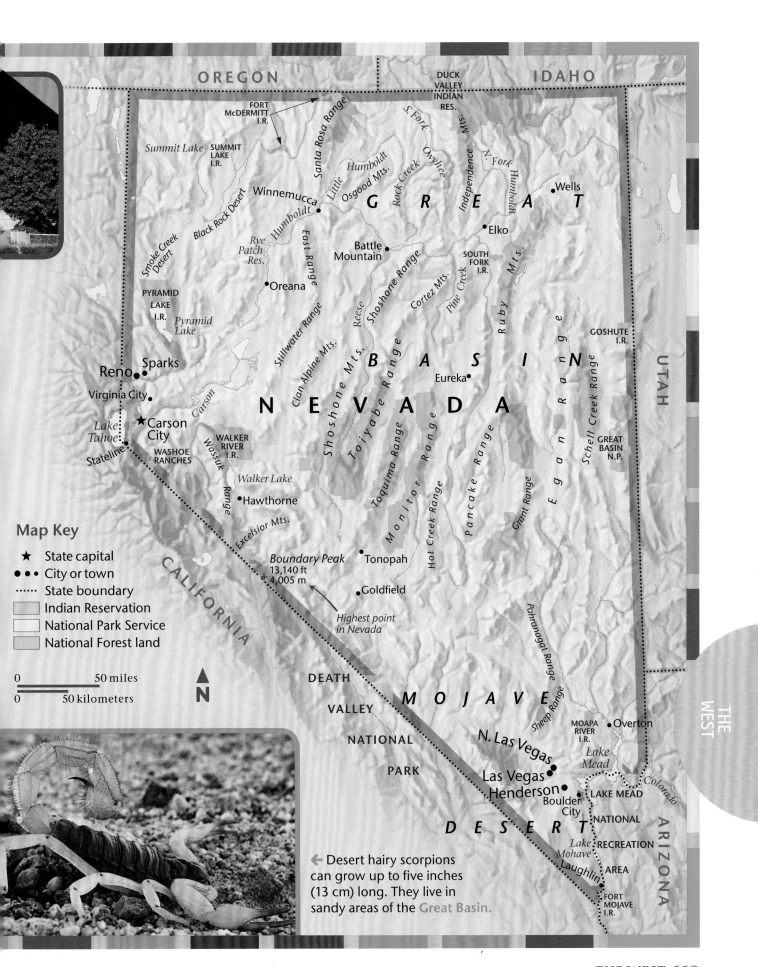

OREGON   DUCK VALLEY INDIAN RES.   IDAHO

FORT McDERMITT I.R.

Summit Lake   SUMMIT LAKE I.R.

Santa Rosa Range

Humboldt

S. Fork

Owyhee

N. Fork Humboldt

Independence Mts.

• Wells

Winnemucca

Little   *Humboldt*

Osgood Mts.

G R E A T

Black Rock Desert

Smoke Creek Desert

Humboldt

Rye Patch Res.

East Range

Battle Mountain

Reese

Shoshone Range

Rock Creek

Cortez Mts.

Pine Creek

SOUTH FORK I.R.

• Elko

Ruby Mts.

Egan Range

GOSHUTE I.R.

UTAH

PYRAMID LAKE I.R.

Pyramid Lake

Stillwater Range

Clan Alpine Mts.

Shoshone Mts.

B A S I N

Schell Creek Range

GREAT BASIN N.P.

• Oreana

Reno • Sparks

N E V A D A

Toiyabe Range

Toquima Range

Monitor Range

Pancake Range

Hot Creek Range

Grant Range

Eureka •

Virginia City •

★ Carson City

Lake Tahoe

WALKER RIVER I.R.

Carson

Wassuk Range

WASHOE RANCHES

Stateline

Walker Lake

Walker Lake

• Hawthorne

Excelsior Mts.

Boundary Peak
13,140 ft
4,005 m

Tonopah •

• Goldfield

*Highest point
in Nevada*

Map Key

★   State capital
• • •   City or town
·····   State boundary
    Indian Reservation
    National Park Service
    National Forest land

0   50 miles
0   50 kilometers

▲ N

CALIFORNIA

DEATH VALLEY NATIONAL PARK

M O J A V E

Sheep Range

Pahranagat Range

MOAPA RIVER I.R.   • Overton

Lake Mead

N. Las Vegas

Las Vegas

Henderson

Boulder City

Lake Mohave

Laughlin

LAKE MEAD

NATIONAL RECREATION

AREA

FORT MOJAVE I.R.

Colorado

ARIZONA

D E S E R T

← Desert hairy scorpions can grow up to five inches (13 cm) long. They live in sandy areas of the Great Basin.

THE WEST

OREGON

The West

Oregon

 Land & Water The Cascade Range, Crater Lake, and the Columbia River are important land and water features of Oregon.

 Statehood Oregon became the 33rd state in 1859.

 People & Places Oregon's population is 4,028,977. Salem is the state capital. The largest city is Portland.

Fun Fact The Bonneville Power Administration, headquartered in Portland, provides about 30 percent of the electricity used in the Pacific Northwest. Most of this power comes from hydroelectric plants along the Columbia River.

STATE OF OREGON

1859

Oregon State Flag

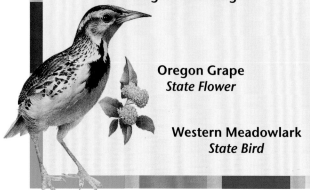

Oregon Grape
State Flower

Western Meadowlark
State Bird

↑ The 125-foot (38-m) Astoria Column near the mouth of the **Columbia River** is covered with scenes of historic events.

↑ The cool, moist climate of the valley of the **Willamette River** is well suited to certain varieties of wine grapes.

↓ Rocky outcrops called sea stacks line Oregon's **Pacific coast**. They are the remains of a former coastline that has been eroded by waves.

PACIFIC OCEAN

COAST RANGES

Astoria

Trask
Tillamook

Newport

Umpqua
Coos Bay
North
Bend
Coos Bay
Coos

Roseburg

Cape
Blanco

Gold Beach

Grants
Pass

Brookings

Illinois

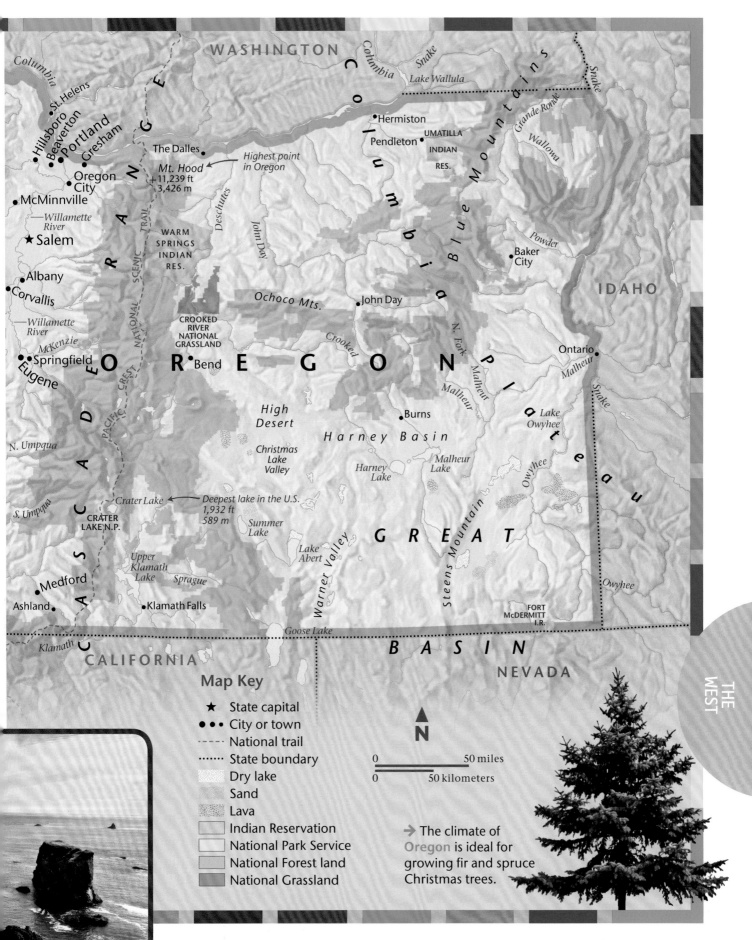

WASHINGTON

Columbia

Columbia
Lake Wallula
Snake
Snake

St. Helens
Hillsboro
Beaverton
Portland
Gresham
Oregon City
McMinnville

Hermiston
Pendleton
UMATILLA INDIAN RES.

Blue Mountains
Grande Ronde
Wallowa

The Dalles
Mt. Hood
+11,239 ft
3,426 m
Highest point in Oregon

—Willamette River

★ Salem

Albany
Corvallis

—Willamette River

McKenzie
Springfield
Eugene

N. Umpqua

WARM SPRINGS INDIAN RES.

Deschutes

John Day

Ochoco Mts.

John Day

CROOKED RIVER NATIONAL GRASSLAND

R· Bend

O R E G O N

Crooked

N. Fork

Powder

Baker City

IDAHO

Ontario

Malheur

Malheur

Malheur

Burns

Harney Basin

N

Plateau

Lake Owyhee

Snake

High Desert

Christmas Lake Valley

Harney Lake

Malheur Lake

Owyhee

S. Umpqua

Crater Lake
Deepest lake in the U.S.
1,932 ft
589 m

CRATER LAKE N.P.

Summer Lake

G R E A T

Owyhee

Steens Mountain

Upper Klamath Lake

Sprague

Lake Abert

Warner Valley

Medford
Ashland

Klamath Falls

FORT McDERMITT I.R.

Klamath

Goose Lake

B A S I N

CALIFORNIA

NEVADA

Map Key

★ State capital
●●● City or town
--- National trail
⋯ State boundary
▦ Dry lake
▦ Sand
▦ Lava
▢ Indian Reservation
▢ National Park Service
▢ National Forest land
▢ National Grassland

↑ N

0   50 miles
0   50 kilometers

→ The climate of **Oregon** is ideal for growing fir and spruce Christmas trees.

CASCADE RANGE

PACIFIC CREST NATIONAL SCENIC TRAIL

Utah

Land & Water
The Great Basin, the Uinta Mountains, and Great Salt Lake are important land and water features of Utah.

Statehood
Utah became the 45th state in 1896.

People & Places
Utah's population is 2,995,919. Salt Lake City is the state capital and the largest city.

Fun Fact
Great Salt Lake is the largest natural lake west of the Mississippi River. The lake, which has a high level of evaporation, is about eight times saltier than the ocean.

↑ Water sports such as inner tubing are popular activities in **Glen Canyon National Recreation Area.**

← A newly married couple stands in front of the Temple in **Salt Lake City,** where Mormons gather for religious ceremonies.

↓ Delicate Arch in **Arches National Park** is one of more than 2,000 arches that have been carved by natural forces over millions of years. The snowcapped La Sal Mountains stand in the distance.

Utah State Flag

Sego Lilly
State Flower

California Gull
State Bird

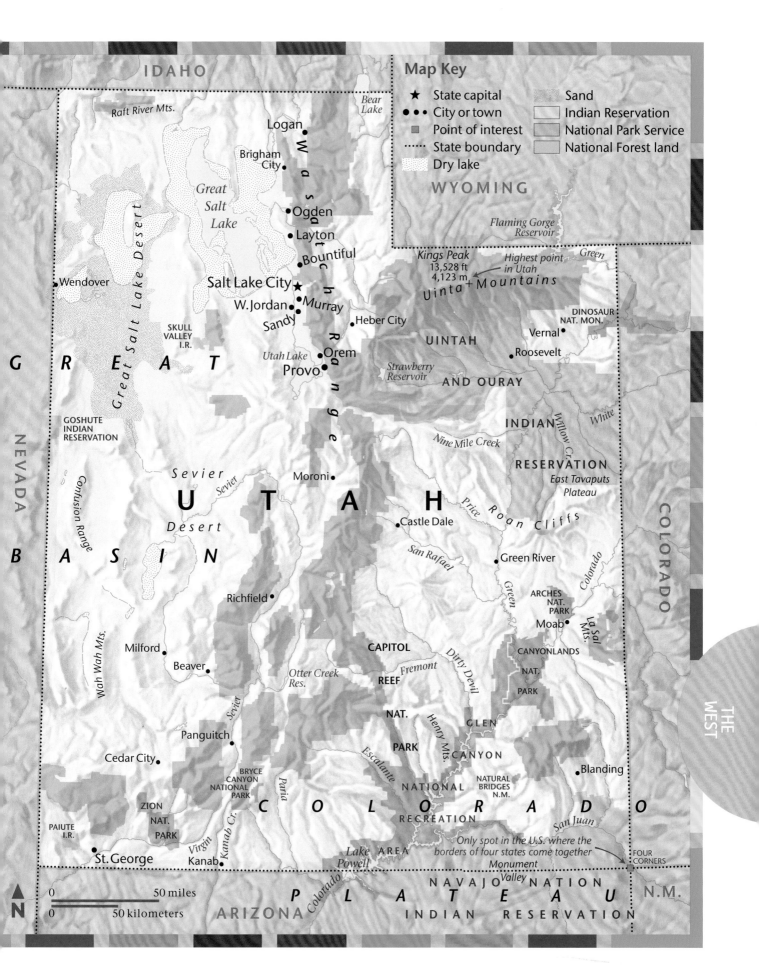

IDAHO

Map Key

★ State capital
• • • City or town
□ Point of interest
· · · · State boundary
Dry lake

Sand
Indian Reservation
National Park Service
National Forest land

WYOMING

Raft River Mts.

Bear Lake

Logan

Brigham City

Great Salt Lake

W a s a t c h   R a n g e

Ogden

Layton

Bountiful

Salt Lake City ★

W. Jordan

Murray

Sandy

Heber City

Utah Lake

Orem

Provo

Wendover

Flaming Gorge Reservoir

Kings Peak
13,528 ft
4,123 m

Highest point in Utah

Green

Uinta + Mountains

DINOSAUR NAT. MON.

Vernal

Roosevelt

UINTAH

Strawberry Reservoir

AND OURAY

SKULL VALLEY I.R.

Great Salt Lake Desert

N E V A D A

G R E A T

B A S I N

GOSHUTE INDIAN RESERVATION

Confusion Range

Sevier

Sevier

Desert

U T A H

Moroni

INDIAN

Willow Cr.

White

RESERVATION

East Tavaputs Plateau

Nine Mile Creek

Price

R o a n   C l i f f s

Castle Dale

San Rafael

Green River

Green

Colorado

COLORADO

ARCHES NAT. PARK

La Sal Mts.

Moab

Richfield

CANYONLANDS

NAT.

PARK

Milford

Wah Wah Mts.

Beaver

CAPITOL

Otter Creek Res.

Fremont

REEF

Dirty Devil

NAT.

Henry Mts.

GLEN

Panguitch

Sevier

PARK

CANYON

Blanding

Cedar City

Escalante

NATURAL BRIDGES N.M.

BRYCE CANYON NATIONAL PARK

Paria

C O L O R A D O

NATIONAL

ZION NAT. PARK

Kanab Cr.

RECREATION

PAIUTE I.R.

Virgin

AREA

Lake Powell

Only spot in the U.S. where the borders of four states come together

FOUR CORNERS

St. George

Kanab

Monument

N.M.

Colorado

N A V A J O   Valley   N A T I O N

0 ___ 50 miles
0 ___ 50 kilometers

N

ARIZONA

P L A T E A U

INDIAN   RESERVATION

San Juan

WASHINGTON

Washington

Land & Water
The Olympic Mountains, the Palouse Hills, and Puget Sound are important land and water features of Washington.

Statehood
Washington became the 42nd state in 1889.

People & Places
Washington's population is 7,170,351. Olympia is the state capital. The largest city is Seattle.

Fun Fact
Mount Rainier, a dormant volcano, last erupted in 1969. Another nearby volcano, Mount St. Helens, erupted in 1980. Winds carried ash from the eruption as far away as Maine.

Washington State Flag

Coast Rhododendron
State Flower

American Goldfinch
State Bird

↑ A Roosevelt elk grazes in the temperate rain forest of **Olympic National Forest**. Adult males weigh up to 1,000 pounds (454 kg).

← The modern skyline of **Seattle** is easily recognized because of its Space Needle tower. The city is an important West Coast port.

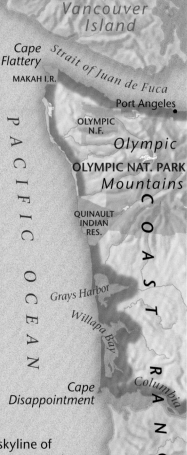

Strait

Vancouver Island

Cape Flattery
Strait of Juan de Fuca
MAKAH I.R.
Port Angeles

OLYMPIC N.F.
Olympic
OLYMPIC NAT. PARK
Mountains

QUINAULT INDIAN RES.

PACIFIC OCEAN

Grays Harbor

Willapa Bay

Cape Disappointment

COAST RANGES

Columbia

0   50 miles
0   50 kilometers

Map Key
★ State capital
●●● City or town
----- National trail
...... State boundary
••••• Country boundary
Glacier
Indian Reservation
National Park Service
National Forest land

CANADA
U.S.

of Georgia

LUMMI I.R.
Bellingham

NORTH

Ross Lake

CASCADES

San Juan Islands

ROSS LAKE N.R.A.

NATIONAL

Skagit

Mount Vernon

PACIFIC CREST NATIONAL SCENIC TRAIL

LAKE CHELAN N.R.A.

PARK

Oak Harbor

Whidbey Island

Okanogan

Republic

Franklin Delano Roosevelt Lake

Colville

CANADA
U.S.

Columbia AREA

NATIONAL RECREATION

Sampoil

KALISPELL I.R.

Omak

COLVILLE

INDIAN

RESERVATION

Colville

Pend Oreille

Port Townsend

TULALIP I.R.

Everett

Lake Chelan

Columbia

Grand Coulee

Banks Lake

LAKE ROOSEVELT

SPOKANE INDIAN RES.

Spokane

OLYMPIC NAT. FOREST

Puget Sound

Skykomish

Kirkland
Redmond
Bellevue
Seattle
Renton

WASHINGTON

Spokane

Spokane Valley

Bremerton

PUYALLUP I.R.

Auburn
Tacoma
Puyallup

Wenatchee

Yakima

Ephrata

Moses Lake

Palouse

Hills

PACIFIC

CREST

★ Olympia

Mt. Rainier 14,411 ft 4,392 m

MT. RAINIER N.P.

Highest point in Washington

Ellensburg

Potholes Reservoir

Pullman

Chehalis

Chehalis

Cowlitz

C A S C A D E

Yakima

Toppenish

YAKAMA

INDIAN

RESERVATION

Columbia Plateau

Yakima

Prosser

Richland

Kennewick

Pasco

Snake

Lake Sacajawea

Pomeroy

Walla Walla

Snake

Blue Mountains

Mount St. Helens

Longview

Vancouver

Goldendale

Columbia

Lake Wallula

IDAHO

OREGON

N

← Tulips are big business in the **Skagit River** Valley, where thousands of these colorful flowers bloom every spring.

↑ An orca swims near the **San Juan Islands**. Also known as killer whales, orcas live in groups called pods.

THE WEST

Wyoming

Land & Water
The Rocky Mountains, Yellowstone National Park, and the Green River are important land and water features of Wyoming.

Statehood
Wyoming became the 44th state in 1890.

People & Places
Wyoming's population is 586,107. Cheyenne is the state capital and the largest city.

Fun Fact
Wyoming is called the Equality State because it was the first state to give women the right to vote, granted in 1869 when it was still a territory.

⬆ Steam and water from Old Faithful Geyser in Yellowstone National Park erupt more than 100 feet (30 m) into the air.

Map Key
★ State capital
•• City or town
⨝ Pass
▪ Point of interest
•••••• State Boundary
•••••• Continental Divide
▢ Indian Reservation
▢ National Park Service
▢ National Forest land
▢ National Grassland

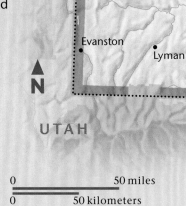

World's first national park, 1872
YELLOWSTONE
Yellowstone Lake
OLD FAITHFUL
NAT. PARK
JOHN D. ROCKEFELLER, JR. MEM. PKWY.
IDAHO
Snake
Teton Range
Jackson Lake
GRAND TETON NATIONAL PARK
• Jackson
Wyoming Range
Green
Bear
Fontenelle Reservoir
FOSSIL BUTTE NAT. MON.
Kemmerer • Hams Fork
Evanston
Lyman
N
UTAH

0   50 miles
0   50 kilometers

Wyoming State Flag

Indian Paintbrush
State Flower

Western Meadowlark
State Bird

← The Wyoming state capitol building in **Cheyenne** was completed in 1890. It is now a U.S. national historic landmark.

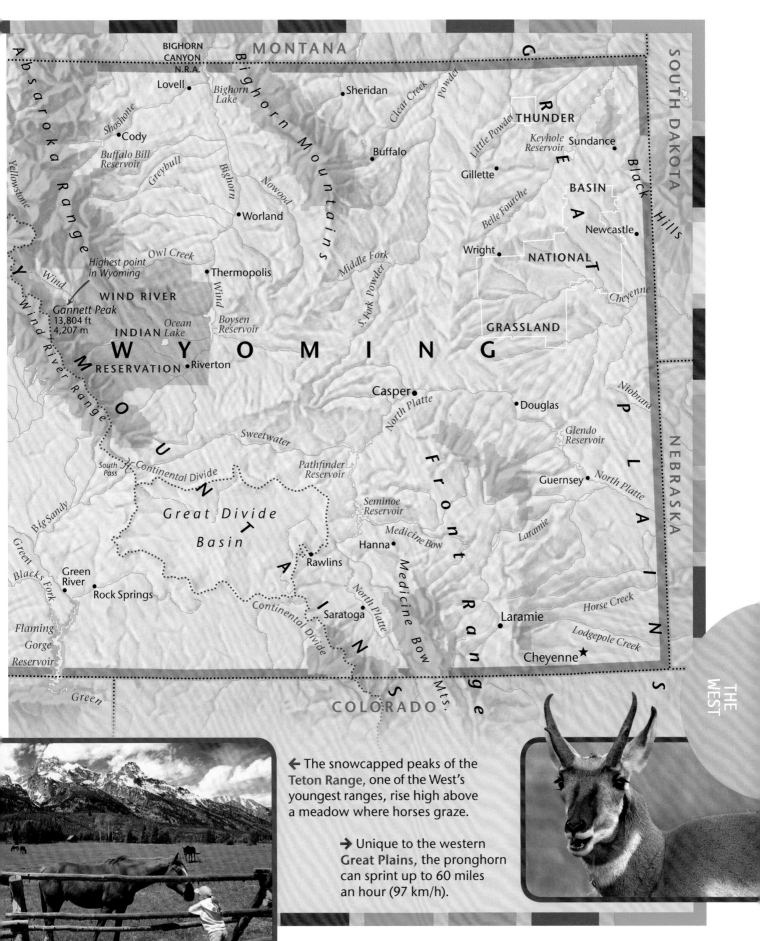

MONTANA

Absaroka Range

BIGHORN
CANYON
N.R.A.

Lovell

Bighorn
Lake

Bighorn Mountains

Sheridan

Clear Creek

Powder

GREAT

THUNDER

Shoshone
Cody

Buffalo Bill
Reservoir

Greybull

Yellowstone

Wind

Highest point
in Wyoming

Gannett Peak
13,804 ft
4,207 m

WIND RIVER

INDIAN

Owl Creek

Bighorn

Nowood

Worland

Wind

Thermopolis

Boysen
Reservoir

Middle Fork

S. Fork Powder

Little Powder

Keyhole
Reservoir

Sundance

Gillette

Belle Fourche

Black Hills

BASIN

Newcastle

Wright

NATIONAL

Cheyenne

W Y O M I N G

GRASSLAND

Wind River Range

Ocean
Lake

RESERVATION

Riverton

Casper

North Platte

Douglas

Niobrara

Glendo
Reservoir

SOUTH DAKOTA

NEBRASKA

South
Pass

Continental Divide

Sweetwater

Pathfinder
Reservoir

Guernsey

North Platte

Big Sandy

Great Divide

Basin

Seminoe
Reservoir

Medicine Bow

Hanna

Laramie

Front Range

Green

Blacks Fork

Green
River

Rock Springs

Rawlins

North Platte

Saratoga

Continental Divide

Medicine Bow

Medicine Bow Mts.

Laramie

Horse Creek

Lodgepole Creek

Cheyenne ★

GREAT PLAINS

Flaming
Gorge
Reservoir

Green

COLORADO

THE WEST

← The snowcapped peaks of the
Teton Range, one of the West's
youngest ranges, rise high above
a meadow where horses graze.

→ Unique to the western
Great Plains, the pronghorn
can sprint up to 60 miles
an hour (97 km/h).

The Territories

The Territories

ACROSS TWO SEAS

Listed below are the five largest* of the fourteen U.S. territories, along with their flags and key information. Two are in the Caribbean Sea; the other three are in the Pacific Ocean. Can you find the other nine U.S. territories on the map?

U.S. CARIBBEAN TERRITORIES

PUERTO RICO

Area: 3,508 sq mi (9,086 sq km)

Population: 3,598,357

Capital: San Juan

Languages: Spanish, English

U.S. VIRGIN ISLANDS

Area: 149 sq mi (386 sq km)

Population: 103,574

Capital: Charlotte Amalie

Languages: English, Spanish or Spanish Creole, French or French Creole

U.S. PACIFIC TERRITORIES

AMERICAN SAMOA

Area: 77 sq mi (199 sq km)

Population: 54,343

Capital: Pago Pago

Languages: Samoan, English

NORTHERN MARIANA ISLANDS

Area: 184 sq mi (477 sq km)

Population: 52,344

Capital: Capital Hill

Languages: Philippine languages, Chamorro, English

OTHER U.S. TERRITORIES

Baker Island, Howland Island, Jarvis Island, Johnston Atoll, Kingman Reef, Midway Islands, Navassa Island, Palmyra Atoll, Wake Island

*Close-up views of the five largest territories are highlighted in enlarged inset maps labeled with a letter. You can see where each territory is by looking for its corresponding letter on the main map.

GUAM

Area: 217 sq mi (561 sq km)

Population: 161,785

Capital: Hagåtña (Agana)

Languages: English, Filipino, Chamorro

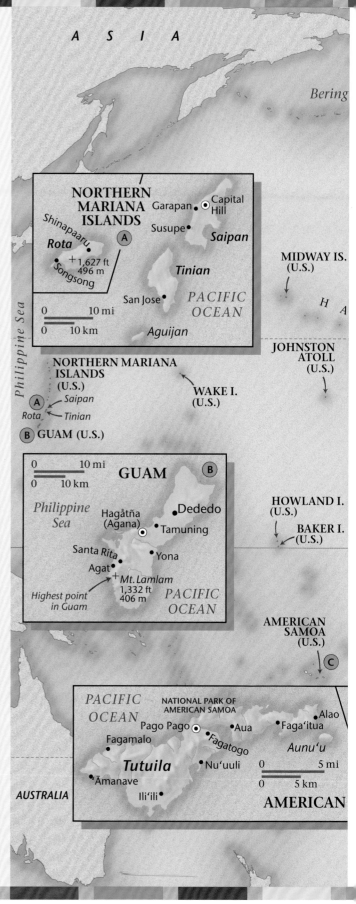

ALASKA

GREENLAND

Sea

N

Map Key

⊛ Country capital
⊙ Territory capital
● ● ● City or town
· · · · Country boundary
National Park Service
National Forest land

0 ——— 1000 miles
0 ——— 1000 kilometers

NORTH

AMERICA

UNITED
STATES

Washington, ⊛
D.C.

ATLANTIC

OCEAN

TROPIC OF CANCER

*Gulf of
Mexico*

NAVASSA
I.(U.S.)

PUERTO
RICO
(U.S.)

U.S.
VIRGIN
IS.(U.S.)

Ⓓ

Ⓔ

Caribbean Sea

KINGMAN REEF
(U.S.)

PALMYRA ATOLL
(U.S.)

W
A
I
I

PACIFIC OCEAN

SOUTH
AMERICA

EQUATOR

JARVIS
I.(U.S.)

Ⓓ

Arecibo

Vega
Baja   Cataño

● San Juan

Carolina

*ATLANTIC
OCEAN*

Aguadilla

Trujillo Alto

Fajardo

Culebra

Mayagüez

PUERTO RICO

Caguas

Cordillera + *Central*
Cerro de Punta
Highest point 4,390 ft, 1,338 m
in Puerto Rico
Ponce

Humacao

Cayey

Guayama

Vieques

0 ——— 20 mi
0 ——— 20 km

Caribbean Sea

ATLANTIC OCEAN

Crown
Mt.
1,556 ft
474 m
+

St. Thomas
⊙ Charlotte Amalie

Cruz Bay

(U.K.)

St. John

VIRGIN
ISLANDS
N.P.

Ⓔ **U.S. VIRGIN
ISLANDS**

0 ——— 20 mi
0 ——— 20 km

Caribbean Sea

St. Croix

Christiansted

Frederiksted

NATIONAL PARK OF
AMERICAN
SAMOA

*PACIFIC
OCEAN*

Ofu

Olosega

Ofu
Olosega

Faleāsao

Ta'ū

Maia

Leusoali'i

Ta'ū
Si'ufaga

NAT. +
PARK OF
AMERICAN
SAMOA

Lata Mountain
3,170 ft
966 m

TROPIC OF CAPRICORN

Ⓒ

SAMOA

Manu'a Islands

THE
TERRITORIES

The United States at a Glance

Land
Five Largest States by Area

1. **Alaska:** 663,267 sq mi (1,717,854 sq km)
2. **Texas:** 268,581 sq mi (695,624 sq km)
3. **California:** 163,696 sq mi (423,972 sq km)
4. **Montana:** 147,042 sq mi (380,840 sq km)
5. **New Mexico:** 121,590 sq mi (314,917 sq km)

Water
Primary Water Bodies Bordering the U.S.

1. **Pacific Ocean:** 65,436,200 sq mi (169,479,000 sq km)
2. **Atlantic Ocean:** 35,338,500 sq mi (91,526,400 sq km)
3. **Arctic Ocean:** 5,390,000 sq mi (13,960,100 sq km)
4. **Gulf of Mexico:** 591,430 sq mi (1,531,810 sq km)

Highest, Longest, Largest

The numbers below show locations on the map.

❶ **Highest Mountain**
Denali (Mount McKinley), in Alaska:
20,320 ft (6,194 m)

❷ **Longest River System**
Mississippi–Missouri: 3,710 mi (5,971 km)

❸ **Largest Freshwater Lake
(entirely in the U.S.)**
Lake Michigan:
22,300 sq mi (57,757 sq km)

❹ **Largest Saltwater Lake**
Great Salt Lake, in Utah:
1,700 sq mi (4,403 sq km)

❺ **Northernmost Point**
Point Barrow, Alaska

❻ **Southernmost Point**
Kalae, Hawai'i

❼ **Easternmost Point**
Sail Rock, West Quoddy Head, Maine

❽ **Westernmost Point**
Peaked Island, Alaska

People

In 2015 more than 320 million people live in the United States. Of these, more than 43 million were born in another country. The largest foreign-born group came from Mexico, followed by India, the Philippines, and China. By 2050 it is estimated that the country's population will approach 400 million, with 72 million being foreign-born.

Five Largest States by Number of People

1. **California:** 39,144,818 people
2. **Texas:** 27,469,114 people
3. **Florida:** 20,271,272 people
4. **New York:** 19,795,791 people
5. **Illinois:** 12,859,995 people

Five Largest Cities* by Number of People

1. **New York, NY:** 8,491,079 people
2. **Los Angeles, CA:** 3,928,864 people
3. **Chicago, IL:** 2,722,389 people
4. **Houston, TX:** 2,239,558 people
5. **Philadelphia, PA:** 1,560,297 people

*Figures are for city proper, not metropolitan area.

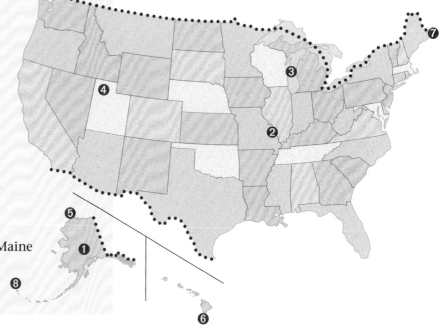

Glossary

Barrier island: a long sandy island that runs parallel to a shore

Bicentennial: the 200th anniversary of an event

Border State: during the Civil War, a slave state that stayed in the Union (Delaware, Kentucky, Maryland, and Missouri)

Boundary: an imaginary line that separates one political or mapped area from another; physical features (such as mountains and rivers) or latitude and longitude lines sometimes act as boundaries

Capital: a place where a country or state government is located

Coniferous forest: needleleaf trees that bear seeds in cones

Container ships: large ships that carry goods in truck-size metal containers among world ports

Contiguous U.S.: the 48 states that are joined together; excludes Alaska and Hawai'i

Continental U.S.: the 49 states located on the continent of North America; excludes Hawai'i

Continental Divide: a natural boundary line separating waters flowing into the Atlantic Ocean and Gulf of Mexico from those flowing into the Pacific Ocean

Creole: a blended language evolved from contact between two or more unrelated languages

Deciduous forests: trees, such as oak, maple, and beech, that lose their leaves in the cold season

Delmarva Peninsula: an East Coast peninsula named for the states it includes: Delaware, Maryland, and Virginia

Desert: a region with either hot or cold temperatures that receives ten inches (25 cm) or less of precipitation a year

Dormant volcano: a volcano that is currently inactive but that may erupt at some time in the future

Erosion: the process by which wind, water, or ice carries away rocks, soil, and other weathered material on Earth's surface

Estuary: the wide part of a river near a sea, where freshwater and saltwater mix

Exports: products made in one place and sent to another to be sold

Foothills: a region of lower hills at the base of a mountain

Fossil: an impression left by the remains of ancient animals or plants that has been preserved in rock or tree sap

Grassland: large areas of mainly flat land covered with grasses

High Plains: flat or gently rolling land above 2,000 feet (600 m); semiarid region east of the Rocky Mountains

Hydroelectric plant: a facility that uses the energy of moving water to create power

Indian reservation: land set aside by the U.S. government for Native Americans to live on and govern

Louisiana Purchase: land purchased from France in 1803 that stretched from the Mississippi River to the Rocky Mountains, and from the Gulf of Mexico to Canada, doubling the size of the country at that time

Mouth: place where a river empties into an ocean or other large body of water

Peninsula: a large piece of land that sticks out into the water

Petroleum: a type of fuel formed when the remains of marine plants and animals are buried beneath sediments and subjected to intense heat and pressure over millions of years

Sedimentary: a kind of rock, such as sandstone, made of small, compressed particles

Shakers: members of a religious group who did not marry and lived in communal societies

Sunbelt: a region of the southern and western U.S. experiencing rapid economic growth and major in-migration of population

Territory: land under the rule of a country but that is not a state or a province of that country

Temperate rain forest: forests found along the Pacific coast of North America where there is a cool, moist climate and where rainfall is abundant

Tropical rain forest: a region occurring mostly in a belt between the Tropic of Cancer and Tropic of Capricorn in areas that have at least 80 inches (200 cm) of rain each year and an average yearly temperature of 77°F (25°C)

Tundra: a region at high latitudes or high elevations that has cold temperatures, low vegetation, and a short growing season

Wetland: land that is covered with or soaked by water; includes swamps, marshes, and bogs

Index

Pictures and the text that describes them have their page numbers printed in **bold** type.

Two-Letter Postal Codes

New Jersey 26–27
New Mexico 92–93
New York **12–13,** 28–29
New York, New York **9, 26, 28–29**
Niagara Falls **12–13**
North Carolina 52–53
North Dakota 80–81
Northern Mariana Islands 122

O

Ohio 82–83
Oil industry **94, 96**
Oklahoma 94–95
Oregon 114–115

P

Peaches **45**
Peanuts **44**
Pennsylvania 30–31
Pigs **64, 68**
Pioneers **71, 78–79**
Potatoes 24, **108–109**
Prairie dogs **78**
Pronghorn **121**
Puerto Rico 122, 123
Pumpkins **9,** 16

R

Rhode Island 32–33
Rice **40**
Rodeos **80**
Roller coasters **26, 82**
Roosevelt, Theodore **81, 84**

S

Sailing **20, 32-33, 86**

Ships **14, 23, 38, 54**
Shrimp **48**
South Carolina 54–55
South Dakota 84–85
Space program **42,** 108
Statue of Liberty **29**
Surfboarding **106–107**

T

Tennessee 56–57
Territories 122–123
Texas **88–89,** 96–97
Tornadoes **94**
Turtles **55, 107**

U

U.S. Virgin Islands 122, 123
Utah **6,** 116–117

V

Vermont 34–35
Virginia 58–59
Volcanoes 106, **106,** 118

W

Washington 118–119
Washington, D.C. 10–11
West Virginia 60–61
Whales 14, **23, 119**
Whitewater rafting **60–61, 90**
Winter sports **24, 32, 35, 86, 105, 110**
Wisconsin 86–87
Wolves **74**
Wyoming 120–121

Two-Letter Postal Codes

ALABAMA.................AL
ALASKA...................AK
ARIZONA.................AZ
ARKANSAS...............AR
CALIFORNIA.............CA
COLORADO...............CO
CONNECTICUT...........CT
DELAWARE...............DE
DISTRICT OF COLUMBIA.....DC
FLORIDA.................FL
GEORGIA................GA
HAWAI'I.................HI
IDAHO..................ID
ILLINOIS................IL
INDIANA................IN
IOWA...................IA
KANSAS.................KS
KENTUCKY...............KY
LOUISIANA..............LA
MAINE..................ME
MARYLAND..............MD
MASSACHUSETTS..........MA
MICHIGAN...............MI
MINNESOTA.............MN
MISSISSIPPI.............MS
MISSOURI...............MO
MONTANA...............MT
NEBRASKA..............NE
NEVADA................NV
NEW HAMPSHIRE.........NH
NEW JERSEY.............NJ
NEW MEXICO............NM
NEW YORK..............NY
NORTH CAROLINA........NC
NORTH DAKOTA.........ND
OHIO...................OH
OKLAHOMA.............OK
OREGON................OR
PENNSYLVANIA..........PA
PUERTO RICO...........PR
RHODE ISLAND..........RI
SOUTH CAROLINA........SC
SOUTH DAKOTA.........SD
TENNESSEE.............TN
TEXAS.................TX
UTAH..................UT
VERMONT..............VT
VIRGINIA..............VA
WASHINGTON...........WA
WEST VIRGINIA.........WV
WISCONSIN.............WI
WYOMING..............WY

Copyright © 2016 National Geographic Partners, LLC

All rights reserved. Reproduction of the whole or any part of the contents without written permission from the publisher is prohibited.

Since 1888, the National Geographic Society has funded more than 12,000 research, exploration, and preservation projects around the world. The Society receives funds from National Geographic Partners, LLC, funded in part by your purchase. A portion of the proceeds from this book supports this vital work. To learn more, visit www.natgeo.com/info.

For more information, visit www.nationalgeographic.com, call 1-800-647-5463, or write to the following address:
National Geographic Partners, LLC
1145 17th Street N.W.
Washington, D.C. 20036-4688 U.S.A.

Visit us online at nationalgeographic.com/books

For librarians and teachers: ngchildrensbooks.org

More for kids from National Geographic: kids.nationalgeographic.com

For information about special discounts for bulk purchases, please contact National Geographic Books Special Sales: ngspecsales@ngs.org

For rights or permissions inquiries, please contact National Geographic Books Subsidiary Rights: ngbookrights@ngs.org

NATIONAL GEOGRAPHIC and Yellow Border Design are trademarks of the National Geographic Society, used under license.

Designed by Jim Hiscott, Jr.

Paperback ISBN: 978-1-4263-2647-9
Hardcover ISBN: 978-1-4263-2434-5
Reinforced library binding ISBN: 978-1-4263-2435-2

Printed in China
16/RRDS/1

Illustrations Credits

Front cover: (background), Brandon Laufenberg/Getty Images; (Sacagawea), Patrick Faricy; (George Washington), Everett Historical/Shutterstock; (boy on rope swing), Corbis; (U.S. globe), ymgerman/iStockphoto; (baseball), Dan Thornberg/Shutterstock; (Seattle Space Needle), Digital Stock; (Route 66 sign), Photodisc; (Lincoln Memorial), Alexander Shor/E+/Getty Images; (cherry pie), BRAND X; (bald eagle), EyeWire Images; (totem pole), Photodisc; (stamp outline), Neftali/Shutterstock; (stamp outline), stamp outline/Shutterstock; **Spine:** (Chrysler Building), Danita Delimont/Getty Images; **Back cover:** (riverboat), Photodisc; (lizard), MWaits/Shutterstock; (lake and mountain), Photodisc; (bald eagle flying), Sekar B/Shutterstock; (hot dog), mj007/Shutterstock

Front matter: 1 (background), Brandon Laufenberg/Getty Images; 1 (UP LE), zschnepf/Shutterstock; 1 (UP RT), Taylor Kennedy/National Geographic Creative; 1 (LO LE), Eric Isselée/Shutterstock; 1 (LO RT), John Kelly/Iconica/Getty Images; 1 (LO CTR), Paul Tillinghast/Getty Images; 2 (LE), Alaska Stock Images/NationalGeographicStock.com; 2 (RT), SergeyIT/Shutterstock; 2 (LO), Rob Byron/Shutterstock; 3 (UP LE), metalstock/Shutterstock; 3 (LO LE), Zuzule/Shutterstock; 3 (UP RT), Eric Isselée/Shutterstock; 3 (CTR), James M Phelps, Jr/Shutterstock; 3 (RT), Geoffrey Kuchera/Shutterstock; 6 (LO LE), erllre74/Shutterstock; 6 (UP RT), Charles Krebs/Riser/Getty Images; 6 (CTR RT), Mike Brake/Shutterstock; 6 (LO RT), James Randklev/Riser/Getty Images; 7, Olivier Le Queinec/Shutterstock; 8 (UP), Billy Hustace/Stone/Getty Images; 8 (LO), sonya etchison/Shutterstock; 9 (LE), Mark R/Shutterstock; 9 (RT), dibrova/Shutterstock; 10 (CTR), PhotoDisc; 10-11 (UP), PhotoDisc; 11 (UP RT), Taylor S. Kennedy/NationalGeographicStock.com; 11 (LO), Jahi Chikwendiu/The Washington Post/Getty Images; **THE NORTHEAST:** 12 (LO), Alaska Stock Images/NationalGeographicStock.com; 12-13, Skip Brown/NationalGeographicStock.com; 14 (UP), Shawn Pecor/Shutterstock; 14 (LO), Donald Gargano/Shutterstock; 15, Joel Sartore/NationalGeographicStock.com; 16 (CTR), Kevin Fleming/Corbis; 16-17 (UP), Jake Rajs/Stone/Getty Images; 16-17 (LO), William S. Kuta/Alamy/Alamy; 17 (UP RT), Catherine Lane/iStockphoto.com; 18 (CTR), Mikael Damkier/Shutterstock; 18 (LO), Jeff Schultes/Shutterstock; 18-19 (UP), PhotoDisc; 19 (LO), Noah Strycker/Shutterstock; 20 (UP), Emory Kristof/NationalGeographicStock.com; 20 (LO), Jeremy Edwards/iStockphoto.com; 21 (UP), Justine Gecewicz/iStockphoto.com; 21 (LO), James L. Stanfield/NationalGeographicStock.com; 22 (UP), Christopher Penler/Shutterstock; 22 (LO), Lijuan Guo/Shutterstock; 23 (LE), Chee-Onn Leong/Shutterstock; 23 (RT), Brett Atkins/Shutterstock; 24 (UP), Paula Stephens/Shutterstock; 24 (CTR), Marcel Jancovic/Shutterstock; 24 (LO), George & Judy Manna/Photo Researchers RM/Getty Images; 25, Tony Campbell/Shutterstock; 26 (UP), Dave Raboin/iStockphoto.com; 26 (CTR), Steve Miller/The Star-Ledger/Corbis; 26-27 (LO), Aimin Tang/iStockphoto.com; 27 (UP), Sheldon Kralstein/iStockphoto.com; 27 (CTR), Andrew F. Kazmierski/Shutterstock; 28 (UP), Cathleen Abers-Kimball/iStockphoto.com; 28-29 (LO), Richard Levine/Alamy; 29 (RT), Glenn Taylor/iStockphoto.com; 30, iStockphoto.com; 31 (LE), Jeremy Edwards/iStockphoto.com; 31 (RT), Racheal Grazias/Shutterstock; 32 (CTR), Mona Makela/Shutterstock; 32 (LO), Joy Brown/Shutterstock; 32-33 (UP), Yare Marketing/Shutterstock; 33 (LO), Robert Kelsey/Shutterstock; 34 (UP), Thomas M Perkins/Shutterstock; 34 (LO), sianc/Shutterstock; 35 (UP), Parker Deen/iStockphoto.com; 35 (LO), rebvt/Shutterstock; **THE SOUTHEAST:** 36 (LO), SergeyIT/Shutterstock; 36-37, Maria Stenzel/NationalGeographicStock.com; 38 (UP), Darryl Vest/Shutterstock; 38 (CTR), Kevin Fleming/Corbis; 38-39 (LO), Wayne James/Shutterstock; 39 (CTR), Ronnie Howard/Shutterstock; 40 (UP), courtesy of the Museum of Discovery, www.museumofdiscovery.org; 40 (LO), Bill Barksdale/Corbis; 41, Travel Bug/Shutterstock; 42 (UP), Wayne Johnson/iStockphoto.com; 42 (LO), NASA; 43 (UP), Varina and Jay Patel/iStockphoto.com; 43 (LO), Valentyn Volkov/Shutterstock; 44 (UP), jackweichen_gatech/Shutterstock; 44 (CTR), Antonio V. Oquias/Shutterstock; 44 (LO), Brian Lasenby/Shutterstock; 45, Andrew F. Kazmierski/Shutterstock; 46 (UP), Leon Ritter/Shutterstock; 46 (CTR), Craig Wactor/Shutterstock; 46 (LO), Anne Kitzman/Shutterstock; 47, Neale Cousland/Shutterstock; 48 (UP), Bob Sacha/Corbis; 48 (CTR), Jim Richardson/Corbis; 48 (LO), J. Helgason/Shutterstock; 49 (LE), Stephen Helstowski/Shutterstock; 49 (RT), Kathryn Bell/Shutterstock; 50 (UP), Vilmos Varga/Shutterstock; 50 (CTR), Daniela Duncan/Getty Images; 50 (LO), Peter Arnold, Inc./Alamy; 51, Mike Flippo/Shutterstock; 52 (LE), Leah-Anne Thompson/Shutterstock; 52 (RT), Forrest L. Smith, III/Shutterstock; 53 (LE), Rob Byron/Shutterstock; 53 (RT), Brad Whitsitt/Shutterstock; 54, Rafael Ramirez Lee/Shutterstock; 55 (UP), Richard Ellis/Getty Images; 55 (LO), Zach Holmes/Alamy; 56 (UP), Envision/Corbis; 56 (LO), Bryan Busovicki/Shutterstock; 57 (LE), Wayne James/Shutterstock; 57 (RT), Jennifer King/Shutterstock; 58 (UP), Darren K. Fisher/Shutterstock; 58 (LO), Travel Bug/Shutterstock; 59 (LE), graham s. klotz/Shutterstock; 59 (RT), Adam Bies/Shutterstock; 60 (CTR), Ken Inness/Shutterstock; 60 (LO), Mary Terribery/Shutterstock; 60-61 (UP), Robert Pernell/Shutterstock; 61 (RT), Adam Bies/Shutterstock; **THE MIDWEST:** 62 (LO), metalstock/Shutterstock; 62-63, Jim Brandenburg/Minden Pictures; 64 (UP), Ralf-Finn Hestoft/Corbis; 64 (CTR), Tim Boyle/Getty Images; 64 (LO), Jenny Solomon/Shutterstock; 65, Kim Karpeles/Alamy; 66 (UP), James Steidl/Shutterstock; 66 (LO), Todd Taulman/Shutterstock; 66 (CTR), john j. klaiber jr/Shutterstock; 66-67 (LO), Melissa Farlow/NationalGeographicStock.com; 68 (UP), jokter/Shutterstock; 68 (LO), Madeleine Openshaw/Shutterstock; 69 (LE), steve schneider/iStockphoto.com; 69 (RT), Andre Jenny/Alamy; 70 (UP), aceshot1/Shutterstock; 70 (LO), Rusty Dodson/Shutterstock; 71, Bruce Dale/NationalGeographicStock.com; 72 (UP), Gary Paul Lewis/Shutterstock; 72 (CTR), Rachel L. Sellers/Shutterstock; 72 (LO), John Brueske/Shutterstock; 73, Cornelia Schaible/iStockphoto.com; 74 (UP), Maxim Kulko/Shutterstock; 74 (CTR), V. J. Matthew/Shutterstock; 74 (LO), Geoffrey Kuchera/Shutterstock; 75, Karla Caspari/Shutterstock; 76 (UP), Neil Phillip Mey/Shutterstock; 76 (LO), Jose Gil/Shutterstock; 77 (LE), Tim Pleasant/Shutterstock; 77 (RT), Rusty Dodson/Shutterstock; 78 (UP), Bates Littlehales/NationalGeographicStock.com; 78-79 (LO), James L. Amos/NationalGeographicStock.com; 79 (UP), Joel Sartore/NationalGeographicStock.com; 79 (LO RT), Jim Richardson/NationalGeographicStock.com; 80 (UP), Ian Martin/NationalGeographicStock.com; 80 (CTR), Randy Olson/NationalGeographicStock.com; 80 (LO), Rusty Dodson/Shutterstock; 81, iofoto/Shutterstock; 82 (UP), aceshot1/Shutterstock; 82 (CTR), Alex Neauville/Shutterstock; 82 (LO), James M Phelps, Jr/Shutterstock; 83, Weldon Schloneger/Shutterstock; 84 (UP), Werner Bollmann/Photolibrary/Getty Images; 84 (CTR), Ira Block/NationalGeographicStock.com; 84 (LO), iofoto/Shutterstock; 85, Danita Delimont/Alamy; 86 (UP LE), Aga/Shutterstock; 86 (UP RT), Brad Thompson/Shutterstock; 86 (CTR), Volkman K. Wentzel/NationalGeographicStock.com; 86 (LO), Alvis Upitis/AgStock Images/Corbis; 87, Layne Kennedy/Corbis; **THE SOUTHWEST:** 88 (LO), Zuzule/Shutterstock; 88-89, Jack Dykinga/NationalGeographicStock.com; 90 (UP), Michael Nichols/NationalGeographicStock.com; 90 (UP), Zschnepf/Shutterstock; 90 (LO), Chris Curtis/Shutterstock; 92 (UP), italianestro/Shutterstock; 92 (CTR), Mariusz S. Jurgielewicz/Shutterstock; 92 (LO), Ralph Lee Hopkins/NationalGeographicStock.com; 94 (UP), Clint Spencer/iStockphoto.com; 94 (LO), Phil Anthony/Shutterstock; 95 (LE), Lindsay Hebberd/Corbis; 95 (RT), MWaits/Shutterstock; 96 (UP), Ben Conlan/iStockphoto.com; 96 (CTR), Mira/Alamy; 96 (LO), Rusty Dodson/Shutterstock; 97, B. Anthony Stewart/NationalGeographicStock.com; **THE WEST:** 98 (LO), Eric Isselée/Shutterstock; 98-99, Gordon Wiltsie/NationalGeographicStock.com; 100 (UP), Benoit Rousseau/iStockphoto.com; 100 (LO), alysta/Shutterstock; 101, Michael Pemberton/Shutterstock; 102 (UP), Stas Volik/Shutterstock; 102 (CTR), Bates Littlehales/NationalGeographicStock.com; 102 (LO), Lindsay Noechel/Shutterstock; 103, Elke Dennis/Shutterstock; 104 (UP), Larsek/Shutterstock; 104 (LO), PhotoDisc; 105, John Kelly/Iconica/Getty Images; 106 (UP), Jim Sugar/Corbis; 106 (LO), Alex Staroseltsev/Shutterstock; 106-107 (UP), jarvis gray/Shutterstock; 107 (UP RT), Steve Raymer/NationalGeographicStock.com; 107 (CTR RT), Jeff Hunter/Photographer's Choice/Getty Images; 108 (UP), Bryan Brazil/Shutterstock; 108 (CTR), Raymond Gehman/NationalGeographicStock.com; 108 (LO), David P. Smith/Shutterstock; 109, Dick Durrance II/NationalGeographicStock.com; 110 (UP), Noah Clayton/The Image Bank/Getty Images; 110 (LO), Doug Lemke/Shutterstock; 111 (LE), Geoffrey Kuchera/Shutterstock; 111 (RT), Jerry Sharp/Shutterstock; 112 (CTR), W. Robert Moore/NationalGeographicStock.com; 112 (LO), Sam Abell/NationalGeographicStock.com; 112-113 (UP), Andy Z./Shutterstock; 113, Danita Delimont/Alamy; 114 (UP), Jennifer Lynn Arnold/Shutterstock; 114 (CTR), Rachell Coe/Shutterstock; 114-115 (LO), Peter Kunasz/Shutterstock; 115 (RT), Tischenko Irina/Shutterstock; 116 (UP), Grafton Marshall Smith/Corbis; 116 (CTR), Nelson Sirlin/Shutterstock; 116 (LO), PhotoDisc; 118 (UP), Natalia Bratslavsky/Shutterstock; 118 (LO), Luis Salazar/Shutterstock; 119 (LE), oksana.perkins/Shutterstock; 119 (RT), Sandy Buckley/Shutterstock; 120 (UP), Videowokart/Shutterstock; 120 (LO), Henryk Sadura/Shutterstock; 121 (LE), Peter Kunasz/Shutterstock; 121 (RT), Nancy Bauer/Shutterstock

RUSSIA

ARCTIC OCEAN

60°N

180°

160°W

140°W

THE WEST
pages 98–121

160°E

40°N

PACIFIC OCEAN

0 _____ 600 miles
0 _____ 600 kilometers

Albers Conic Equal-Area Projection

180°

20°N

THE WEST
pages 98–121

160°W

140°W